BIJANITA

Authentic Indian Cuisine

ANITA BASAK

Working Title Publishing

Bijanita Authentic Indian Cuisine by Anita Basak

First edition

ISBN 1-59344-900-3 soft cover

Imprint: Working Title Publishing
        Galt, California   USA
Website: www.workingtitlepublishing.com
Email: workingtitlepublishing.com@earthlink.net

My Mother's Kitchen

Throughout my life, Bijanita's kitchen was located in Hull, England, Bronx, NY, Plainview, NY, Coudersport, PA and Rochester, NY. Although the scenery changed, the venue was always the same. The kitchen was the heart and soul of our home, my mother's stage. I reminisce about many weekend mornings when we would have friends and family around the kitchen table engaging in "ahada" (idle conversation), while my mother confidently produced an elaborate breakfast spread.

When I arrived home from school each day, my mother was in the kitchen preparing the family meal. As I did my homework, and my father read the newspaper, she was creating chicken korma and aloo gobi, or on a rainy afternoon, kirchuri. It is still amazing to me to recall the simplicity with which she planned, shopped, and prepared a meal. She was never distracted by all the commotion; she never used a script or fancy kitchen instruments. Her hands were the implements of portion. She was so comfortable with creating meals, she had performed the scene over and over; her efforts always led to a standing ovation of the pallet.

My husband, David, reminisces about his first introduction to Bengali cuisine: the occasion when he accepted an invitation to dinner at our home. He grew up on what I refer to as the classic bland diet, consisting of white bread, white meat, and mashed potatoes. My mother, of course, prepared a colorful array of dishes and treated her guests as royalty. She served each course with care, and patiently awaited that request for a second serving. My boyfriend, at that time, ate like he was starving. He reflects back on this occasion as the birth of his taste buds, his first step into being part of a Bengali family.

It was several years later, still with David, that I traveled to India for my wedding. In Calcutta, my grandmother greeted her to-be grandson-in-law with the same grace my mother had provided. She expressed her emotion through food, the ultimate portal to the heart. My future husband and my grandmother bonded without the need for words. By enjoying her cooking, he showed his respect for her and for that, she respected him. It was then that I realized this routine had been a success for many years, although now across continents. My mother obviously completed her apprenticeship at a very young age with my grandmother, as she orchestrated the same performance. My grandmother created talented dishes as she squatted near a coal stove with a cornucopia of spices she ground with mortar and pestle. Bengali cooking does not require you to be on the floor, unless you are into the true tradition.

I have visited India frequently since the age of five. During my childhood, I did not have an appreciation for the complex mix of spices typically used in Bengali cuisine. My grandmother would prepare a special meal for me, consisting of steaming hot parathas and plum chutney. She would wait until I was ready for dinner and then prepare parathas for me one by one. I still recall my grandmother catering to each person's schedule and patiently waiting until the last family member ate before she would consider eating herself. In fact, if one of her children, of which she had many, did not arrive home for the family meal, she would not eat until their arrival.

It is my grandmother, my mother's mentor, who passed on her passion for creating meals and being a gracious hostess to friends and family. It is these treasures that my mother shares graciously with you. Enjoy, and create your own impressions. Bengali food is not fast food, it takes patience and caring; it communicates love, without words.

Madhumita Basak-Smith

Over the past 3 decades, my mother dictated all of her recipes to me and as she did so, I would jot down her thoughts. My father had an old IBM typewriter and I proceeded to type all of those recipes that were used for her cooking classes, and in her cooking for family and friends. My mother and I sat down and divided the recipes into an album and compiled them by hand. I hope that these lovely recipes will find warm remembrance in everyone's hearts and homes.

Mohua (Basak) Poddar

With this book, my mother is sharing her secrets; secrets that have nourished our immediate and extended family as well as scores of family and friends. I have no doubt that you will enjoy scrumptious meals from this book; but use these secrets to help you savor milestones in your life and create fond memories for your family and yourself. My mother has fed generations of Basaks, but more importantly, she fostered an environment – surrounding each and every meal – that celebrates the bonds that weave families and friends together. As you make these recipes your own, please know that they come from a special woman who has touched thousands of lives with her warmth and love. I hope you can do the same…with the secrets that are in here!

Amit Basak

I would like to thank Linda Dilworth for her patience and persistence in editing and revising my recipes. I appreciate her scrutinizing each and every recipe, because I like to cook without measuring utensils, so you can imagine the task Linda had.

A special mention goes to Gayle E. Macdonell, for capturing my childhood home in India, for the cover of this book. She was able to depict the origin of all these recipes…. my mother's kitchen.

Finally, I want to thank my friends and family for encouraging me with their appetites.

Anita Basak

Dedicated to my beloved husband, the late *Dr. Bijan Kumar Basak*

The successful completion of this book was possible due to my greatest inspiration in life, my husband, Dr. Bijan Kumar Basak. It was his desire to entertain friends and family with elegant parties, luscious meal creations, and good conversation. Any good food central in our home was due to his presence.

He would joke when I got up in the morning and went directly to the kitchen. Out of delight, he sometimes would call me the "*maida meye*" - the baker girl. He needed to have something special, like dessert, before going to bed. It was his sweet tooth that provided the strongest impetus for me to be creative in making desserts such as zilapy, payesh, and rash malai; desserts unique to Bengal. Soon after he retired, the tantalizing journey of "my cooking" became "our cooking." He became a treasured companion in the kitchen. He was always eager to learn. He joyfully watched how mixing various spices and using selective cooking vessels made a difference in taste.

It was my husband's idea and motivation to share and spread all the cooking skills that I had accumulated over time. This was the beginning of my offering Indian cooking classes both at home and at the Cornell Boces Adult Education Center. The help and support that I received from my husband and children were the precursor to the publication of this book with its wide collection of recipes. I thank my husband dearly for all his appreciation, feedback, and suggestions during our 42 years of marriage.

This book serves as a memorable finale to our marriage, which was full of his incredible energy and love as a spectacular connoisseur of food. As Indian food is becoming more and more popular in this country, I hope that a broad range of people will choose this authentic Bengali cookbook.

Anita Basak

11

Table of Contents

Menus   pgs 203 -- 209

SPICES AND CONDIMENTS

Asafoetidahing (Hing)
Bay Leaves
Cardamom
Cinnamon
Chili
Cilantro Leaves (Coriander)
Cloves
Coriander
Cumin, Black Cumin
Fennel Seeds
Fenugreek
Garlic
Ghee
Ginger
Mint
Mustard Seeds, Red Mustard Seeds
Nutmeg
Poppy Seeds
Saffron
Turmeric
Peppercorns

Anita's Masala Powder

2 cups whole cumin
½ cup black peppercorns
½ cup bay leaves
10 – 12 dried whole red chilies

In a frying pan, on low heat, combine all of the above spices and roast. When spices begin to smell as though they have been smoked, cool for 1 hour on a dish. Process in a spice grinder (a coffee grinder will do).

Garam Masala Powder

2 cups Anita's masala powder
½ cup ground cinnamon
½ cup cardamom powder

Combine

Chutney Masala

2 Tbsp. whole cumin
2 Tbsp. whole black cumin
2 Tbsp. fenugreek
2 Tbsp. fennel seeds
2 Tbsp. red mustard seeds

Combine

Chutney Masala Powder

2 Tbsp. whole cumin
2 Tbsp. whole black cumin
2 Tbsp. fenugreek
2 Tbsp. fennel seeds
2 Tbsp. red mustard seeds

In a frying pan, on low heat, combine all of the above spices and roast. When spices begin to smell as though they have been smoked, cool for 1 hour on a dish. Process in a spice grinder (a coffee grinder will do).

ALMOND BERFEE

Ingredients

½ cup water
2 cups sugar
½ cup butter
2 cups non-fat dry milk
1 lb. peeled, ground almonds
½ tsp. almond extract

Directions

In a heavy sauce pan, boil water and sugar to make thick syrup. Add butter and mix until butter is melted into the syrup. Add dry milk and ground almonds. Stir mixture briskly so it does not become lumpy. After 1 – 2 minutes mixture will become thick. Remove from heat and add almond extract. Pour mixture into a greased an 8 x 8 inch pan. Spread and flatten to ½ inch thick. When Berfee has cooled, cut into diamond-shaped pieces. Serve this delicious candy chilled. Almond Berfee will keep in the refrigerator for a month.

ALOO CHOPS
(Potato Patties)

Ingredients

2 Tbsp. oil
1 cup chopped onions
1 tsp. grated fresh ginger root
$^1/_8$ tsp. compounded asafoetida (hing)
1 tsp. whole cumin
1 large green chili pepper, chopped
½ tsp. red pepper
1 tsp salt
4 large potatoes, boiled and mashed
1 Tbsp. lemon juice
2 tsp. garam masala powder

Batter Ingredients

1 cup graham flour or chick pea flour (may substitute tempura mix)
¼ cup corn starch
1 tsp. whole black cumin
1 tsp. salt
¼ tsp. baking soda (eliminate if using tempura mix)
$^1/_8$ tsp. crushed red pepper
1 cup water
2 cups oil

Directions

Heat oil in large skillet and fry onions, ginger, hing, cumin, chili peppers, red pepper and salt until onions are golden brown. Add potatoes, lemon juice and garam masala and mix well. Allow to cool, and then shape thick, 2 inch diameter patties.

In a small bowl mix all batter ingredients except for oil. Use only enough of the water to achieve the consistency of pancake batter. Dip patties in batter and deep fry in the 2 cups of hot oil until golden brown.

This is a delicious vegetarian dish or appetizer.

ALOO PARATHA

Dough Ingredients

3 cups whole wheat (chapati) flour
2 cups all purpose flour
1 tsp. sugar
1 tsp. salt
¼ tsp. baking soda
4 Tbsp. oil
½ cup milk
1 ½ cups hot water

Filling Ingredients

8 medium potatoes, peeled
1 tsp. salt
water, enough to cover potatoes
1 large onion, finely chopped
2 green chilies, finely chopped
1 tsp. salt
2 Tbsp. Anita's bhaja masala
1 tsp. red chili powder
1 Tbsp. lemon juice
½ cup finely chopped cilantro leaves
½ cup white flour
1 cup oil, mixed with 2 Tbsp. of ghee

Directions

In a large bowl mix the flours, sugar, salt, baking soda and oil with hands. Slowly add milk while mixing. Then add a small amount of water at a time while mixing, just until dough comes away cleanly from sides of the bowl. Shape into a large ball and cover with a damp cloth and let rest for 1 – 2 hours.

Boil potatoes in salted water until soft. Drain and mash with a potato masher. Let cool.

Heat oil in a small fry pan. Add onion, green chilies and salt, sauté until lightly browned. Then add Anita's bhaja masala and red chili powder. Pour this mixture over mashed potatoes, then add lemon juice and cilantro. Mix well with hands, then form 20 balls out of filling mixture.

Form another 20 balls out of dough. Flatten each ball into the palm of your hand. Make a bit of an indentation at the center and place a potato ball on the indent. Pull the dough sides up and secure around potato ball. Flatten slightly and set aside. Form all 20 similarly.

Sprinkle a flat surface with flour and roll each paratha ball into a thin 9 inch round. Heat a skillet on medium. Place paratha rounds into the pan, coat evenly with ½ tsp. of ghee mixture, turn and coat other side. Continue turning several times with a flat spoon for about 2 minutes. Dough will puff then turn crispy.

This bread can be served hot with any Indian chutney, sweet or sour as preferred.

ALOO-KOPI-R DALNA
(Cauliflower and Potato Curry)

Ingredients

½ cup oil
1 large head of cauliflower, cut into pieces
3 tsp. salt
1 tsp. whole cumin
4 large potatoes, cut into 1 inch cubes
1 large onion, chopped
2 tsp. turmeric powder
1 tsp. chili powder
1 tsp. cumin powder
1 Tbsp. grated fresh ginger root
2 medium tomatoes, chopped or ½ cup tomato sauce
1 16 oz. package of fresh or frozen peas
1 cup water
fresh cilantro as garnish
2 fresh green hot chilies, chopped

Directions

Heat oil in a large skillet. When just beginning to smoke, add whole cumin to skillet and fry for 30 seconds. Add cauliflower and 1 tsp. salt and sauté until light brown. Transfer cauliflower with slotted spoon to a separate bowl, leaving remaining oil in skillet. Add potatoes and onion and fry until lightly browned. Add remaining spices along with grated ginger, remaining salt and tomatoes. Stir frequently until spices are well incorporated. Add peas, sautéed cauliflower and water. Cover skillet and continue simmering vegetables on low until cooked through.

Garnish with fresh cilantro leaves and chilies. This vegetarian dish can be served with rice pillau or Indian naan bread.

ALOO-POSTO WITH GREEN SPRING ONIONS
(Potato and Poppy Seed)

Ingredients

1 cup poppy seeds
½ cup water
½ cup oil
1 tsp. whole black cumin
6 potatoes, cut 1" lengths, ¼" thick
2 tsp. salt
½ tsp. chili powder
¼ tsp. turmeric powder
1 bunch spring onions, cut into 1" pieces
3 green chilies, sliced
1 tsp. Anita's masala powder

Directions

Add poppy seeds to a blender with water and blend until smooth in order to form a paste.

Heat oil in a deep frying pan until just beginning to smoke. Add cumin, after 30 seconds add potatoes. Brown the potatoes for a few minutes. Add salt, chili powder, turmeric powder. Stir for 1 minute. Add spring onions and mix well. Cover the pan for 2 minutes. Once the spring onions become tender and mix well with potatoes, add poppy seed paste and sliced green chilies. Cook well for about 3 – 4 minutes. Sprinkle garam masala on top. Remove from heat and place in a serving dish.

This is an authentic Bengali dish which is wonderful for Sunday lunch. It is served with Karai Dhal (muge dhal).

BALUSHAI

Ingredients

4 cups flour
1 cup butter
1 tsp. baking soda
$^1/_8$ tsp. ground nutmeg
2 cups yogurt
4 cups sugar mixed with ½ cup hot water
½ cup water
4 cups vegetable shortening

Directions

Mix flour, butter, baking soda and nutmeg by hand. Add yogurt and ½ cup hot water mixture and mix until soft dough forms. Let dough sit at room temperature. Divide dough into 28 – 30 plum sized balls. Make an indentation into the middle of each ball. Heat shortening in a deep frying pan and fry 8 – 10 balushais on low heat until golden brown. Each side should be fried for 2 – 3 minutes. Remove with a slotted spoon onto paper towel.

In a saucepan, add sugar and ½ cup water. Bring to a boil and simmer to a thickness similar to maple syrup consistency.

While balushais are still hot, place a few at a time into prepared syrup. Syrup consistency should be similar to maple syrup thickness and must be very hot. Lift balushais out and place on a platter. They should be generously glazed and are delicious with coffee.

For additional flavor, add a few cinnamon sticks to the hot syrup.

BHAPA SALMON FISH
(Cooked in Steam)

Ingredients

4 – 6 salmon steaks
1 large onion, cut into pieces
1 large tomato
2 garlic cloves
2" piece of fresh ginger root, peeled
½ cup olive oil
Foran (few pieces each of whole cardamom, cinnamon stick, bay leaves and 1 tsp. whole cumin)
2 Tbsp. sugar
1 tsp. turmeric powder
1 tsp. chili powder
1 tsp. coriander powder
½ tsp. ground cinnamon
2 tsp. salt
2 tsp. Anita's masala powder
½ cup plain yogurt
2 – 3 green chilies, sliced
¼ cup chopped cilantro leaves

Directions

Place fish on a baking dish. To a food processor add onion, tomato, garlic and ginger and finely chop.

In a medium sized pan, heat oil until just beginning to smoke. Add foran and sugar. Stir and then add onion mixture to pan. Fry for 2 – 3 minutes then add turmeric powder, chili powder, coriander powder, ground cinnamon, salt, Anita's masala powder and yogurt. Cook for 3 – 4 minutes for a paste to form. Spread the paste over fish, coating well.

In the meantime, place a large tray of water in the oven and bring to a boil. Tightly cover baking dish containing the fish with aluminum foil. Place the baking dish on a rack over the boiling water and bake for 20 – 30 minutes at 350°. Add water to boiling pan as necessary.

Remove fish from oven and allow steam to dissipate before removing foil. After removing foil, garnish with chili slices and chopped cilantro. This bhapa fish is served in Bengal on special occasions. Serves 4.

BHINDI BHAJI
(Fried Okra)

Ingredients

2 Tbsp. oil
½ tsp. whole cumin
2 large onions cut into small pieces
2 large potatoes cut into small pieces
1 lb. okra, each cut into 4 pieces
1 fresh tomato, chopped
½ tsp. turmeric powder
1 tsp. cumin powder
½ tsp. crushed red pepper
2 tsp. salt

Directions

Heat oil until just beginning to smoke in large skillet then add whole cumin, onion and potato. Sauté for a few minutes. Add remaining ingredients and continue cooking on low heat until potatoes are cooked through and moisture is absorbed. Be careful to keep vegetables whole and not mashed.

BLACK MUGE DHAL
(Lentils with Cream Sauce)

Ingredients

2 cups black muge (lentils)
8 cups water
¼ cup ghee
4 large tomatoes, chopped or ¾ cup tomato sauce
2 tsp. grated fresh ginger root
2 tsp. sugar
2 tsp. salt
1 tsp. chili powder
1 tsp. garam masala powder
½ cup heavy cream

Directions

Wash lentils well and cook in 8 cups of water for about 1 hour (until lentils are almost mushy).

In a small frying pan, melt ghee then add remaining ingredients except for the cream. Fry for 2 – 3 minutes. Add to lentils and cook for an additional 20 minutes stirring frequently. Add the heavy cream and serve warm. This dish is delicious served with rice or nan bread.

BUTTERED CHICKEN

Chicken Ingredients

4 lbs chicken legs and thighs
4 garlic cloves
2 Tbsp. grated fresh ginger root
2 tsp. chili powder
2 tsp. coriander powder
1 tsp. cumin powder
2 tsp. tandoori masala powder
1 tsp. garam masala powder
1 tsp red food coloring
1 tsp. yellow food coloring
4 Tbsp. plain yogurt
2 Tbsp. vinegar
2 Tbsp. oil
2 tsp. salt
1 large onion, sliced
Lemon slices

Directions

Peel skin off chicken, wash and set aside. Place all remaining ingredients (except onion and lemon slices) into a blender and blend at medium speed until well mixed. Dip chicken pieces, one by one, into the mixture and lay on a baking sheet. Refrigerate for about 1 day to marinate.

Preheat oven to 400° and bake 35 – 40 minutes or until well cooked. If barbecue is preferred, follow same instruction, but grill chicken for about 15 minutes each side. Decorate this delicious dish with fresh onions and lemon slices.

Sauce Ingredients

½ cup butter
1 tsp. sugar
1 tsp. salt
½ tsp. chili powder
2 cups tomato sauce
1 ½ cups heavy cream
1 cup water
2 fresh green chili peppers, sliced (do not use dried chilies)
2 Tbsp chopped fresh cilantro leaves

Directions

Melt butter in a sauce pan. Add sugar and salt stirring until well dissolved. Add chili powder and tomato sauce. Cook until tomato sauce seems to separate from butter, about 5 – 10 minutes. Stirring, slowly add cream and water to mixture. Bring to a boil and simmer 5 more minutes.

Lay prepared chicken in a baking dish and cover in sauce. Bake covered in 350° oven for 15 – 20 minutes before serving. Sprinkle with green chili peppers and cilantro.

Serving 6 – 8, this dish is excellent served with buttered rice and naan.

BUTTERFLY CHICKEN CUTLET

Ingredients

3 – 4 lbs. chicken drumsticks, skinned
2 large onions, grated
4 garlic cloves, grated
2 tsp. grated fresh ginger root
4 Tbsp. lemon juice
2 tsp. salt
1 tsp. chili powder
1 ½ tsp. garam masala
¼ tsp. turmeric powder
3 – 4 egg whites
3 cups bread crumbs
2 cups oil

Directions

Split drumsticks lengthwise. Carefully separate the meat from the bone keeping the tail end of the bone attached. Chop off the remainder of the bone. Flatten the meat with a meat tenderizing mallet, will resemble the shape of a butterfly.

Combine onion, garlic, ginger, lemon juice, salt, chili powder, garam masala and turmeric. Add the meat and marinate in the refrigerator for 4 – 6 hours.

Beat egg whites, dip the cutlets in them one at a time. Pour bread crumbs on a platter. Each cutlet should be well coated with bread crumbs. Set on a plate and cover well. Heat oil in a frying pan. Fry 2 or 3 cutlets at a time on medium heat, about 1 – 1 ½ minutes per side until golden brown.

Serve on a platter with a crisp salad.

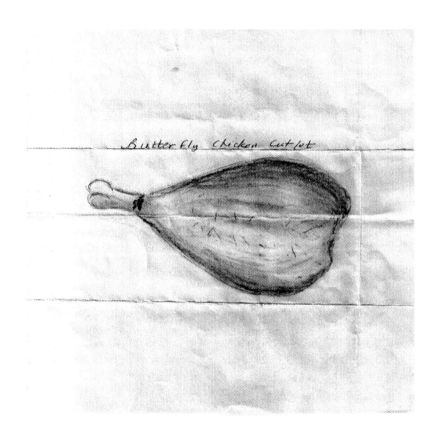

Butter fly Chicken Cutlet

BUTTERFLY SHRIMP CUTLET

Ingredients

1 lb. jumbo shrimp
1 large onion, grated
2 tsp. salt
2 tsp. lemon juice
½ tsp. turmeric powder
1 tsp. grated fresh ginger root
1 tsp. chili powder
1 tsp. garam masala powder
1 large egg, lightly beaten
2 cups bread crumbs
2 cups oil

Directions

Peel shrimp and wash well. Split shrimp backs lengthwise and flatten with a meat tenderizer. In a large bowl, combine onion, lemon juice and all spices. Add shrimp, stir well to coat and marinate over night.

Heat oil in a large skillet. Dip shrimp into egg then coat in breadcrumbs. Fry slowly until golden brown.

CABBAGE BHAJI

Ingredients

$^1/_3$ cup oil
1 bay leaf
½ tsp. whole cumin
Few pieces whole cardamom
Few pieces cinnamon stick
4 large potatoes, cut into 8 pieces each
1 lb. fresh peas or 1 pkg. frozen peas, thawed and drained
½ tsp. chili powder
1 tsp. grated fresh ginger root
2 tsp. turmeric powder
1 tsp. cumin powder
2 fresh tomatoes or ½ cup tomato sauce
2 tsp. sugar
1 Tbsp. salt
1 head cabbage, shredded
½ tsp. garam masala powder
1 tsp. ghee

Directions

In a large frying pan, heat oil until just beginning to smoke. Add bay leaf, whole cumin, cardamom, cinnamon stick and sauté until browned. Add potatoes and fry until lightly browned. Add fresh peas (if frozen, add after cabbage), chili powder, grated ginger, turmeric powder, cumin powder, tomatoes, sugar and salt. Mix well and sauté. Add cabbage and mix well. Simmer, stirring thouroughly, until cabbage is soft. Remove from heat and add garam masala powder and ghee.

CARROT HALOOWA

Ingredients

2 lbs. grated fresh carrots
1 gallon milk
3 cups sugar
½ cup ghee
½ cup sliced almonds
½ tsp. saffron
½ tsp. cardamom powder

Directions

Add carrots and milk to a large pan. Bring to a boil and cook on low heat until milk is absorbed into the carrots. A thick paste will form. Add sugar and ghee. Stir frequently making sure paste doesn't stick to the bottom of the pan. Add almonds and saffron, continuing to cook until quite thick. Spread into a greased pan, leveling to 1 inch thickness. Sprinkle with cardamom powder, cool and cut into squares. Serve warm or cold for dessert.

CAULIFLOWER AND POTATO CHECHKI

Ingredients

½ cup oil
1 tsp. whole black cumin
1 cauliflower head, cut into 1 inch pieces
2 potatoes, cut into cubes
2 tsp. salt
½ tsp. chili powder
¼ tsp. turmeric powder
½ cup water
2 green chilies, sliced
1 tsp. Anita's bhaja masala powder

Directions

In a deep frying pan, heat the oil until just beginning to smoke. Sprinkle black cumin into oil and fry for 30 seconds. Add cauliflower, potato and salt. Fry on medium heat until golden. Add chili powder, turmeric and water. Cover and continue to cook for 5 minutes. When potatoes and cauliflower are tender, add green chili and bhaja masala. Stir the mixture while continuing to cook for an additional 5 minutes until vegetables are browned. Serve this cauliflower dish with hot luchis.

CAULIFLOWER IN COCONUT-MUSTARD SAUCE

Ingredients

½ cup oil
1 tsp. whole black cumin
2 large potatoes, each cut into 8 pieces
1 large head of cauliflower, flowerets only
1 tsp. sugar
1 tsp. crushed chili pepper
2 tsp. grated fresh ginger root
½ cup grated fresh coconut
1 tsp. turmeric powder
2 tsp. salt
1 large tomato, chopped or ¼ cup tomato sauce
2 Tbsp. blended mustard (prepared)
1 cup water
1 tsp. ghee
Green chili pieces
Cilantro leaves

Directions

Heat oil and cumin in a large sauce pan. When seed start to jump, add potatoes and cauliflower. Stir until cauliflower is lightly browned. Add sugar. Then add chili pepper, ginger, coconut, turmeric and salt. Add tomato and continue stirring for a few minutes. Mix mustard with water and add to cauliflower. Check to see if potatoes are done (potatoes take longer to cook and may be precooked slightly so cauliflower won't over cook. It should retain its crispness). When cooking is complete, add ghee and pieces of green chili and coriander leaves (optional) before serving.

Note: if substituting flaked baking coconut for fresh, omit sugar.

CHICKEN CHOPS

Ingredients

2 lbs. chicken breast
4 large potatoes
2 cups + 2 Tbsp. oil
2 large onions, chopped
2 garlic cloves, grated
1 tsp. grated fresh ginger root
1 fresh green chili, sliced
½ tsp. turmeric powder
1 tsp. cumin powder
½ tsp. chili powder
1 tsp. sugar
Salt to taste
2 Tbsp. tomato sauce
2 tsp. lemon juice
2 eggs
¼ cup raisins
Bread crumbs
2 tsp. garam masala powder

Directions

Place chicken in a large pot and fill with enough water to cover chicken. Boil chicken until meat begins to separate from the bone. Remove chicken from pot, de-bone and mash. Add potatoes to pot of water and boil until soft. Mash potatoes and set aside.

In a small frying pan, heat 2 Tbsp. oil and fry the onions and garlic until golden brown. Add ginger, sliced chili, turmeric, cumin powder and chili powder and fry for 1 minute. Add sugar, salt and tomato sauce. Add mashed chicken and mix well. Add lemon juice, mashed potatoes and garam masala into the mixture. Mix well and form into slightly flattened balls.

Beat eggs in a small bowl. Dip each ball in egg then dredge in bread crumbs. Heat 2 cups oil and deep fry each chop until golden brown. Serve hot with sweet chili sauce and cucumber salad.

CHICKEN CUTLET

Ingredients

4 lbs chicken breasts
1 large onion, grated
4 garlic cloves, grated
2 Tbsp. lemon juice
2 tsp. grated fresh ginger root
½ tsp. turmeric powder
2 tsp. garam masala powder
½ tsp. chili powder
1 tsp. cumin powder
2 tsp. salt
1 tsp. sugar
2 eggs, well beaten
Bread crumbs
Oil

Directions

Flatten chicken breasts with a meat tenderizing mallet. Mix the next 10 ingredients in a large bowl, add chicken and marinate for 6 – 8 hours.

Dip each cutlet into the beaten eggs. Pour bread crumbs on a platter. Each cutlet should be well coated with bread crumbs. Heat oil and deep fry chicken over low heat until golden brown in color. Serve hot with rice pillau.

CHICKEN IN YOGURT

Ingredients

3 large onions, grated
4 garlic cloves, grated
2 tsp. grated fresh ginger root
½ cup oil
Few pieces bay leaves, cinnamon sticks and cardamom pods
3 tsp. sugar
1 Tbsp. salt
1 tsp. chili powder
3 lbs. chicken pieces
1 cup yogurt
2 Tbsp. sour cream
½ tsp. saffron
½ cup hot water
1 ½ tsp. Anita's garam masala
2 tsp. coriander powder
1 tsp. ghee

Directions

In a medium bowl, combine grated onions, garlic and ginger.

In a large frying pan, heat oil until just beginning to smoke. Add pieces of bay leaves, cinnamon and cardamom and fry for 30 seconds. Add grated onion mixture and fry until lightly browned. Add sugar, salt and chili powder and mix well. Add chicken pieces and fry for 20 – 25 minutes or until oil separates from onions and spices. Add yogurt, sour cream, saffron and ½ cup hot water, and then bring to a boil. Cover pan and simmer for 20 minutes until chicken is cooked, then add Anita's garam masala, and ghee. Cover again and turn off heat.

If raisins are desired, add golden raisins with yogurt. Serve with rice or pillau.

CHICKEN KORMA

Ingredients

½ cup plain yogurt
2 tsp. turmeric powder
4 tsp. salt
4 – 5 lbs. chicken parts, skinned and washed
½ cup oil
1 tsp. whole cumin
A few pieces of cardamom, cloves, cinnamon stick, peppercorns and bay leaf
4 onions, finely chopped
6 cloves garlic, grated
2 tsp. grated fresh ginger root
2 tsp. sugar
1 tsp. chili powder
2 tsp. coriander powder
2 large tomatoes, chopped or ½ cup tomato sauce
2 cups water
1 tsp. garam masala powder
¼ cup sour cream
2 tsp. ghee
2 – 3 hard boiled eggs, chopped
Fresh cilantro leaves

Directions

Mix yogurt with 1 tsp. of the turmeric and 2 tsp. of the salt. Pour over chicken parts, stir and let marinate for 1 hour. Then in a large heavy sauce pan, heat oil to point of just beginning to smoke and add all of the whole spices. Add onion, garlic and ginger. Sauté to golden brown. Then add sugar, remaining salt and all powdered spices except for the garam masala. Mix for one minute.

Add tomatoes (or sauce) and continue stirring until oil separates from mixture. Add marinated chicken. Continue cooking on medium heat, stirring to prevent sticking to the pan. When the chicken begins to absorb the sauce, add water and bring to a boil. Lower heat, cover and simmer for about 20 minutes. When chicken is nicely tender but not yet falling apart, add garam masala powder, sour cream and ghee. Garnish with hard boiled eggs and cilantro. Serve with fluffy rice. Serves 6 – 8.

CHICKEN MADRAS STYLE

Ingredients

½ cup oil
2 Tbsp. red mustard seeds
2 – 3 bay leaves
4 large onions, chopped
4 garlic cloves, grated
2 tsp. grated fresh ginger root
1 tsp. sugar
4 tsp. salt
2 tsp. coriander powder
2 tsp. turmeric powder
1 tsp. chili powder
1 large tomato, sliced
4 lbs. chicken, skinned and cut into small pieces
½ cup poppy seeds and ½ cup fresh coconut processed in a blender
½ cup water
2 tsp. ghee
1 tsp. garam masala powder

Directions

In a large pot, heat oil until just beginning to smoke. Add mustard and bay leaves and cook until seeds begin to pop. Add onions, garlic, ginger, sugar and salt. Once onions have browned, add coriander powder, turmeric powder, chili powder, tomato and chicken and fry for about 10 minutes. Add the poppy seed and coconut mixture, water, ghee and garam masala. Cook covered on low heat for about 10 more minutes.

CHICKEN MAKHANI

Ingredients

3 – 4 lbs. chicken breast, cut into small cubes
2 tsp. salt
2 Tbsp. vinegar or lemon juice
1 cup yogurt
3 tsp. tandoori masala powder
1/2 cup oil
2 Tbsp. butter
1 tsp. whole cumin
A few pieces of bay leaves
2 large onions, chopped
3 - 4 cloves of garlic, crushed
1 Tbsp. grated fresh ginger root
1 tsp. chili powder
1 tsp. coriander powder
2 cups half & half
1 tsp. garam masala powder
1/2 cup fresh cilantro, chopped
3 green chilies, sliced

Directions

Marinate chicken in 1 tsp. salt, vinegar, yogurt and 1 tsp. tandoori masala for 3 - 4 hours.

In a deep frying pan, heat oil, butter, whole cumin and bay leaves. Add onions, garlic and ginger. Stir while frying for 3 - 4 minutes. Add 1 tsp. salt, chili powder, coriander powder, and remaining tandoori masala powder. Fry these ingredients for 3 - 4 minutes. Place the marinated meat into the mixture and cook on medium heat. Stir frequently so the meat does not stick to the bottom of the pan. After 10 minutes add half & half and garam masala powder. Cook for 2 - 3 more minutes. Remove from heat, garnish with cilantro and chilies and serve immediately.

CHICKEN MALABUR

Ingredients

½ cup poppy seeds, soaked overnight
1 cup grated fresh coconut
½ cup water
1 cup oil
Few pieces of bay leaves
1 tsp. whole cumin
2 tsp. sugar
2 tsp. grated fresh ginger root
4 garlic cloves, crushed
2 cups chopped onions
1 tsp. turmeric powder
2 tsp. coriander powder
1 ½ tsp. chili powder
2 tsp. salt
2 large tomatoes, chopped
4 – 5 lbs. chicken legs, thighs or breasts, skinned and fat removed
1 tsp. garam masala powder
1 Tbsp. ghee
½ cup fresh cilantro leaves

Directions

Add soaked poppy seeds, grated coconut and water to a blender and process. Set mixture aside.

In a large pot, heat oil until just beginning to smoke. Add bay leaves and cumin, brown a bit. Add sugar, ginger, garlic and onions. Sauté until lightly browned. Then add turmeric, coriander, chili powder, salt and tomatoes. Continue to cook until a thick sauce forms and the oil separates out. Add chick parts, stirring occasionally for about 20 minutes. Pour coconut-poppy seed mixture and garam masala powder into pot, cover and simmer for 10 – 15 minutes more or until chicken is done.

Before serving add ghee and sprinkle with cilantro. This maglay (royal) dish is excellent served with any Indian bread.

CHICKEN MASALA

Ingredients

4 lbs. chicken, skinned and cut into pieces
½ cup oil
4 large onions, sliced
6 – 8 garlic cloves, grated
2 tsp. turmeric powder
1 tsp. chili powder
2 tsp. grated fresh ginger root
½ cup tomato sauce or 4 fresh tomatoes, chopped
1 Tbsp. salt
1 tsp. sugar
4 tsp. garam masala powder
2 tsp. ghee
Green chilies
Fresh cilantro

Directions

In a large pot, add chicken and enough water to cover. Boil for about 10 minutes and set aside.

In another large pot, heat oil until just beginning to smoke and fry onions and garlic until golden brown. Add all other ingredients, except garam masala and ghee. Fry for 1 – 2 minutes. Remove chicken from 1st pot, reserving stock, and add to 2nd pot with sauce. Stir frequently while continuing to cook for about 15 minutes. If the chicken looks dry, add 1 cup of the chicken stock. Add garam masala and ghee.

Garnish dish with fresh green chilies and cilantro.

CHICKEN PASANDA

Ingredients

3 lb. chicken, well trimmed of skin and surface fat
½ cup thick yogurt
2 tsp. salt
1 tsp. turmeric powder
1 tsp ground red pepper
1 cup oil
4 large bay leaves
8 cardamom pods
6 cups chopped onion
4 garlic cloves, finely minced
1 2" piece of fresh ginger root, finely grated
2 tsp. sugar
½ cup skinless blanched almonds + 1 cup milk blended
   together to make a thick paste
2 tsp. garam masala powder
2 tsp. ghee
fresh cilantro, chopped

Directions

In a large bowl combine chicken, yogurt, salt, turmeric powder and ground red pepper. Mix well, cover and marinate in refrigerator for a few hours or over night.

Heat oil in a heavy pan and add bay leaves and cardamom pods. Then add chopped onion, garlic, ginger and sugar. Cook, stirring often, until the mixture is nicely browned. This may take 25 minutes or longer and care must be taken so that the mixture does not stick or burn. Add marinated chicken, stir well and add water. Cover the pan, cook about 15 – 20 minutes or just long enough so the chicken pieces are cooked without drying or breaking.

Add the blended almond mixture, garam masala and ghee. Remove from heat and let stand until ready to serve. You can reheat briefly before serving. Garnish with fresh cilantro.

CHICKEN-DO-PIAZA

Ingredients

2 – 3 lbs. whole chicken
4 Tbsp. oil
2 pieces of bay leaf
4 cardamom pods
2 – 3 pieces of cinnamon stick
4 large onions, cut into small pieces
6 garlic cloves, grated
2 large tomatoes, sliced
1 tsp. sugar
2 tsp. salt
1 tsp. chili powder
1 ½ tsp. turmeric powder
2 tsp. coriander powder
1 tsp. ginger paste
2 cups warm water
1 tsp. garam masala powder
1 tsp. ghee
½ cup chopped cilantro leaves

Directions

Cut whole chicken into 8 pieces. In a large pan, heat oil until just beginning to smoke then fry bay leaf, cardamom pods and cinnamon stick for 30 seconds. Add onions and garlic continuing to cook until lightly browned. Add tomatoes, sugar, salt, chili powder, turmeric powder, coriander powder and ginger paste. Fry until the mixture is reduced to a paste, about 10 minutes. Add the chicken pieces and fry another 10 minutes. Add warm water and cover the pan. Let boil on low heat for 20 minutes. When chicken is tender, add the garam masala powder and ghee. Keep warm until ready to serve. Garnish with cilantro leaves.

This dish should be served with rice pillau for 4 – 6.

CHINGRI LAAU
(Shrimp with Italian Light Green Squash)

Ingredients

1 lb. medium shrimp, deveined and cleaned
½ cup olive oil
½ tsp. garlic salt
1 tsp. whole black cumin
A few bay leaves
2 – 3 green chilies
1 large potato, cut into cubes
1 Tbsp. grated fresh ginger root
½ tsp. chili powder
½ tsp. turmeric powder
1 large tomato, chopped
2 Tbsp. salt
1 Tbsp. sugar
1 large Italian light green squash (laau), skinned and cut into
 ¼ inch pieces
½ cup freshly crushed coconut
Cilantro leaves

Directions

In a medium sized skillet sauté shrimp with a small amount of the oil and the garlic salt until pink. Immediately remove the shrimp and set aside. Add the remaining oil to the skillet. Sprinkle the black cumin, bay leaves and green chilies into the heated oil. Add the potatoes and ginger and stir for a few minutes. Add the remaining spices, tomato, salt and sugar. Fry for an additional 2 minutes. Add the squash (laau), cover and continue cooking on medium heat for 5 more minutes. Add the crushed coconut and shrimp.

Cook for a few more minutes, until vegetables are soft. Sprinkle with cilantro leaves before serving.

CHOLAR DHAL WITH COCONUT
(Channa Dhal)

Ingredients

2 cups cholar dhal
4 cups water
2 tsp. salt
¼ tsp. baking soda
½ cup light olive oil
Foran (1 tsp. whole cumin, 2 - 3 pieces bay leaves, 4 – 6 pieces cardamom, 3 – 4 cinnamon sticks broken into small pieces)
½ whole fresh coconut, shelled and cut into small pieces
1 Tbsp. sugar
2 tsp. grated fresh ginger root
½ tsp. turmeric powder
1 tsp. chili powder
2 tsp. Anita's roasted masala powder
2 large tomatoes, chopped
1 tsp. ghee
2 green chilies, sliced
½ cup chopped cilantro leaves

Directions

Thoroughly wash cholar dhal. Add to a medium sized pan along with water, salt and baking soda. Bring to a boil on high heat. Then lower heat to a simmer, cover and cook until the dhal is soft enough to mash with a spoon.

In a small frying pan, heat olive oil until just beginning to smoke. Add all of the foran spices and coconut and fry until coconut pieces are lightly browned. Then add sugar, ginger, turmeric, chili powder, Anita's masala powder and tomato. Cook this until mixture becomes a paste, about 2 minutes.

Add the cooked paste to the cholar dhal in a pan. Cook for 4 – 5 minutes on low heat, stirring well to incorporate the paste into the dhal. Add ghee.

Garnish with green chilies and cilantro before serving. This delicious dhal can be served along with plain white rice, naan or chapati. The nutritional value of the dhal is comparable to that of a full meal. Serves 8 – 10.

CHOPPED CUCUMBER SALAD

Ingredients

2 whole cucumbers, peeled and finely chopped
2 whole tomatoes, finely chopped
1 cup chopped cilantro
½ cup chopped jalapeno
4 Tbsp. sugar
1 tsp. salt
1 lime

Directions

Combine first 4 ingredients in a serving bowl. Add next 3 ingredients. Squeeze the lime onto the salad and mix well. Serve as a side dish with Aloo Chops.

COCONUT BERFEE

Ingredients

1 fresh coconut, grated
8 oz. container of whole milk ricotta cheese
2 cups sugar
1 cup non-fat dry milk
½ tsp. cardamom powder

Directions

Cook first 4 ingredients until thick enough to form balls, stirring constantly to prevent burning. Add cardamom powder then cool and form balls. Serve with coffee.

COCONUT SHANDESH

Ingredients

2 cups half & half
2 fresh coconuts, grated
4 cups sugar
Cardamom seeds removed from pods and ground to powder

Directions

In a large pot bring 1 cup of half & half to a boil. Lower heat and continue to cook until thickened. Blend 1 cup half & half and grated coconut in a blender. Add coconut mixture to thickened half & half. Cook briskly and add sugar. Continue to cook until thickened, partially covering pot with a lid to prevent spattering.

Pour into square dish while mixture is warm. Sprinkle cardamom powder on top. Let cool. Cut into 1 inch square pieces.

CURRIED EGGS

Ingredients

½ cup oil
12 hard boiled eggs
2 large onions, grated
2 cloves of garlic, grated
2 tsp. grated fresh ginger root
1 large tomato, finely chopped
1 tsp. turmeric powder
1 tsp. chili powder
1 tsp. coriander powder
1 tsp. garam masala powder
Salt to taste
2 tsp. sugar
½ cup yogurt
1 cup water

Directions

In a medium sized pan, heat oil and lightly brown eggs. Slice them in half and place in a baking dish cut side up. Set aside.

In the same pan, sauté the onion, garlic and ginger. Add remaining ingredients except for yogurt and water and continue frying until a nice sauce forms. Then add yogurt and cool for about 1 minute. Add water and bring to a boil. Pour over eggs and bake in 350° oven for 10 minutes. Serve with fluffy rice.

DAHI RAITA WITH CUCUMBER

Ingredients

4 cucumbers, peeled and grated
2 tsp. salt
4 tsp. sugar
1 cup plain yogurt
½ cup sour cream
1 tsp. Anita's spice
cilantro for garnish

Directions

Mix grated cucumber with salt and place into a calendar. Allow to drain for 15 minutes.

In a serving bowl, mix together sugar, yogurt and sour cream with a fork. Add cucumber to mixture, sprinkle with Anita's spice and garnish with cilantro.

DHAI MACH
(Fish Cooked in Yogurt)

Ingredients

2 - 3 lbs. salmon steak or white stripe bass steak
1 ½ tsp. salt
½ tsp. turmeric powder
2 Tbsp. oil
2 tsp. ghee
1 large onion, crushed
1 Tbsp. ginger paste
1 Tbsp. sugar
2 Tbsp. whole garam masala
1 tsp. chili powder
½ tsp. coriander powder
2 tsp. garam masala powder
¼ tsp. nutmeg
1 cup yogurt
½ cup sour cream
4 - 5 garlic cloves, chopped
2 - 3 green chilies

Directions

Marinate the fish with salt, turmeric, crushed garlic. In medium sized skillet heat the oil and ghee. Sauté onion, ginger, sugar and whole garam masala pieces. Place the fish on top of ingredients. Cook each side about 1 minute. Move the fish to one side of the pan. Add chili powder, coriander powder, garam masala powder, and nutmeg. Fry these spices for 3 - 4 minutes with onions. In the meantime mix the yogurt and sour cream together. Pour into spice mixture. Spread the fish into the sauce and then cover. Simmer for 5 minutes. Top with green chilies. This fish is delicious with fluffy white rice.

DHOKAR DALNA

Ingredients

3 cups channa dhal, soaked overnight in warm water
1 ½ cups olive oil
¼ tsp. hing (Asafoetida)
2 tsp. turmeric powder
2 tsp. chili powder
2 tsp. cumin powder
2 Tbsp. ginger paste
3 Tbsp. salt
Whole spices (bay leaves, 2 pieces of dry red chili, few cardamom pods, 1 tsp. whole cumin and 1 cinnamon stick broken into pieces)
4 potatoes, cut into small pieces
1 tsp. sugar
2 tomatoes, chopped
½ cup yogurt
3 cups water
2 tsp. Anita's bhaja masala powder
2 tsp. ghee
cilantro leaves
green chilies

Directions

Process soaked dhal in a food processor until a paste is formed. The paste should not be quite smooth. Place channa dhal paste into a mixing bowl.

In a small saucepan, heat ½ cup oil, hing, 1 tsp. turmeric powder, 1 tsp. chili powder, 1 tsp. cumin powder, 1 Tbsp. ginger paste and 1 Tbsp. salt. Fry together and pour into bowl with channa dhal paste. Mix well. Pour into greased 9" x 12" baking dish. Place into oven at 350° for 30 – 40 minutes. Inserted knife should come out clean and will have a browned crust. Cool, then cut into 1" squares.

Heat ½ cup oil in a flat frying pan and fry pieces until golden brown. Remove to a serving dish.

In a deep frying pan, heat remaining oil until just beginning to smoke. Add whole spices and fry for 30 seconds. Add potatoes and fry until lightly browned. Remove potatoes to a separate bowl. Add sugar and remaining ginger, salt, chili powder, cumin powder and turmeric powder. Stir spices for 1 minute. Add tomatoes and yogurt. Stir mixture for 3 – 4 minutes. It will become a sauce. Add 3 cups of water and bring to a boil. Place potatoes into the sauce. When potatoes are soft, add Anita's bhaja masala powder and ghee. Remove from heat. Pour sauce over channa dhal pieces in serving dish. Let soak, then garnish with cilantro leaves and green chilies.

EGGPLANT BEGÚN VARTHÁ

Ingredients

2 eggplants, peeled and cut into large chunks
Salted water
2 Tbsp. ghee or oil
1 large onion, chopped
2 tomatoes, chopped
Salt to taste
2 tsp. sugar
1 tsp. garam masala powder
1 tsp. grated fresh ginger root or ginger powder
1 fresh green chili, chopped or chili powder (optional)
fresh cilantro leaves

Directions

Boil eggplant in salted water until soft. Mash eggplant like a potato.

In a skillet, heat ghee or oil then add onion and fry until lightly browned. Add mashed eggplant, tomato, salt to taste, sugar, garam masala powder, ginger and chili. If using chili, it is recommended to use only part, not whole chili. Cook 5 – 6 minutes while stirring. Should be creamy and soft when done. Garnish with fresh cilantro leaves.

FISH CHOPS

Ingredients

2 lbs. potatoes, boiled in skin, peeled and mashed.
1 tsp. salt
1 tsp. lemon juice
2 tsp. garam masala powder
2 Tbsp. oil
½ cup chopped onion
1 tsp. fresh grated garlic
1 tsp. grated fresh ginger root
1 tsp. whole cumin
1 lb. fish, boiled and flaked (2 small cans of tuna may be substituted)
1 tsp. chili powder
2 tsp. ginger powder
½ tsp. turmeric powder
2 tsp. sugar
1 Tbsp. tomato sauce
½ cup raisins
1 beaten egg
Bread crumbs
2 cups oil

Directions

Mix mashed potatoes with salt, lemon juice and 1 tsp. garam masala. Set aside.

In a frying pan, heat 2 Tbsp. oil until just beginning to smoke. Fry onions, garlic, fresh ginger and cumin until golden brown. Add fish, rest of spices, sugar, tomato sauce and raisins. Sauté gently until mixture becomes quite dry. It must be dry enough to be rolled into a firm ball.

Take egg sized portions of potato mixture into the palm of your hand. Flatten out and place about a plum sized ball of fish mixture into the center of potato mix. Enclose fish in the potato mix and carefully roll between the palms of your hands to make a smooth egg shaped form. Dip in the beaten egg and roll in bread crumbs. Fry in oil until golden brown.

FISH CUTLET

Ingredients

2 lbs. fish fillet (any white fish such as cod, flounder, sole, etc.)
1 large onion, grated
1 tsp. grated fresh ginger root
1 tsp. green chili peppers
¼ cups white vinegar
1 tsp. garlic powder
1 tsp. garam masala powder
Salt to taste
1 egg, beaten
2 cups unseasoned bread crumbs
2 cups oil

Directions

Combine onion, ginger, chili peppers, vinegar, garlic powder, garam masala powder and salt. Marinate the fish in this mixture overnight or for several hours.

Dip each piece of fish in beaten egg and coat in bread crumbs. Heat oil and deep fry each piece until golden brown. Serve on a platter garnished with tomatoes and cucumbers.

FISH KALIYA

Ingredients

2 lbs. Halibut or striped bass, cut into 4" pieces
2 tsp. salt
1 ½ tsp. turmeric powder
½ tsp. garlic powder
½ cup oil
Foran (2 bay leaves, a few cardamom pods and cinnamon stick and 1 tsp. whole cumin)
2 onions, grated
2 garlic cloves, crushed
2 Tbsp. ginger paste
2 tomatoes, cut into pieces
1 tsp. red chili powder
1 tsp. coriander powder
1 cup water
2 tsp. garam masala powder
1 tsp. ghee
2 fresh green chilies, sliced
½ cup fresh cilantro leaves

Directions

Clean fish pieces and rub 1 tsp. salt, ½ tsp. turmeric, ½ tsp. garlic powder and mix well with the fish pieces. In a large frying pan, heat oil until just beginning to smoke. Set fish into the hot oil and fry until both sides are golden brown. Remove fish from pan one piece at a time with slotted spoon. Set aside on a platter.

Add foran to oil remaining in pan. Stir for a few seconds, then add onion, garlic and ginger pastes along with 1 tsp. salt and fry until golden brown. Then add tomato pieces and remaining powdered spices except the garam masala. Cook this mixture for 2 – 3 minutes then add 1 cup of water and bring to a boil. Add fried fish to this sauce, cover and simmer for 2 – 3 more minutes. Add garam masala powder, ghee, green chilies and coriander leaves.

This dish is an eastern India favorite often served during festivities and special occasions with rice and pillau. Serves 4 - 6.

FISH WITH MUSTARD

Ingredients

2 – 3 lbs. Tilapia, cleaned and cut into 1 ½" slices
2 tsp. salt
½ tsp. garlic powder
½ tsp. turmeric powder
¼ cup olive oil
Foran (1 tsp. black cumin)
1 small tomato, sliced
1 tsp. red chili powder
1 cup red mustard seeds, soaked in 1 cup water to form a paste
3 – 4 green chili slices

Directions

Marinate the fish with salt, garlic powder and turmeric.

Heat the oil in a medium frying pan until just beginning to smoke. Add the black cumin and fry for 40 seconds. Place the fish onto the heated oil in pan, then turn. In one corner of the pan, add tomato and red chili powder, mix and cook for 1 minute. Pour the mustard paste over the fish and mix the fried spices over the fish. Cover the pan and simmer for 4 – 5 minutes. Fish should be well covered with mustard sauce.

Garnish with green chilies and serve with plain white rice. Serves 4 – 5.

FRENCH CUT BEANS WITH POTATOES AND MUSTARD SAUCE

Ingredients

2 Tbsp. oil
1 tsp. whole black cumin or mustard seed
2 tsp. salt
4 large potatoes cut like French fries
1 tsp. turmeric powder
1 tsp. sugar
½ tsp. chili powder
1 lb. French cut string beans
1 cup water
2 Tbsp. mustard mixed with 1 cup water

Directions

Heat oil in a frying pan then add cumin seed, salt and potatoes. After frying for a short time, add turmeric, sugar and chili powder. Add string beans, stir well and continue cooking for a few minutes. Cover pot and let simmer 5 minutes. Add mustard and continue simmering until vegetables are done.

Homemade mustard can be prepared by soaking ½ cup mustard seeds in 1 cup hot water. Blend in a blender to make a thin paste.

FRIED POTATO STICKS

Ingredients

2 medium potatoes, peeled and sliced small like toothpicks
½ tsp. salt
Oil for deep frying

Directions

Rub potato sticks with salt. Deep fry in oil until golden brown. Remove sticks from oil with a slotted spoon and drain on paper towel.

Fried potato sticks are to be spread over Spicy cat fish roast dish and served with any beer or wine. Fried potato sticks are excellent served with fish cutlets, chicken cutlets or as a side dish to cooked dhal.

GAJA

Ingredients

2 lbs. self-rising flour
3 cups sugar
¼ tsp. salt
1 tsp. whole black cumin
2 sticks unsalted butter, melted
2 cups warm water, as needed
4 cups shortening
1 tsp. sugar
1 cup water

Directions

Combine self-rising flour, sugar, salt, cumin and melted butter. Mix well until it resembles dry crumbled dough. Add warm water gradually until the dough looks like pastry dough. Do not overwork. Roll out dough on a floured surface until 1/2 inch thick. Cut into rectangular 1" x 2" pieces.

In a frying pan, heat the shortening on medium heat until melted. Fry the rectangular pieces on very low heat until each side is golden brown. Turn the pieces very gently. They will be crispy and flaky. Remove them with a slotted spoon onto a paper towel. Fry remaining pieces in the same manner. In the meantime boil the sugar with one cup water until a thick syrup forms. Gently place 2 cooked pieces on a slotted spoon, one on top of the other. With another spoon pour syrup 3 to 4 times over top of the pieces. Allow the syrup to drain. Place the sugarcoated rectangular pieces on a platter. Continue with the rest of the pieces in the same manner. The sugar will crystallize over the tops. Serve with tea or coffee.

GROUND MEAT GHUGNY

Ingredients

½ cup oil
4 large potatoes
1 tsp whole cumin
2 small dried red chilies
2 whole bay leaves
4 large onions, chopped
2 garlic cloves, grated
1 can tomato sauce or 4 fresh tomatoes
1 Tbsp. turmeric powder
2 tsp. chili powder or 1 tsp. fresh green chili, chopped
2 tsp. coriander powder
2 tsp. grated fresh ginger root
4 tsp. salt
2 tsp. sugar
2 ½ cups water
2 lbs. any ground meat
3 cans chick peas, drained
2 tsp. ghee
2 tsp. garam masala powder
4 tsp. lemon juice

Directions

Heat oil in a skillet and lightly brown potatoes. Remove potatoes and set aside. Add whole cumin, whole red chilies and bay leaves, then brown. Add chopped onions and grated garlic. Fry until lightly browned. Then add potatoes again along with tomato sauce, turmeric, chili powder, coriander, ginger, salt and sugar. Fry until sauce is well mixed.

At the same time, steam the chopped meat with ½ cup of water in a skillet. When cooked drain meat and add to sauce along with chick peas. Continue to fry for 5 – 10 minutes. Then add 2 cups water and cover pan. Simmer for 5 more minutes. Add ghee, garam masala and lemon juice.

This can be served with rice or any kind of bread. Serves 6 –8.

GULAB JAMUN

Ingredients

1 16 oz. container ricotta cheese
3 cups non-fat dry milk
1 cup Bisquick®
¼ tsp. baking soda
½ cup unsalted butter, softened
¼ tsp. cardamom powder
4 cups sugar
6 cups water
3 cups shortening

Directions

Mix ricotta cheese, non-fat dry milk, Bisquick, baking soda, butter and cardamom by hand so the dough becomes smooth and well mixed. Cover with a wet towel and refrigerate for one hour.

In saucepan make clear syrup with sugar and water. Boil the syrup for about 15 – 20 minutes. Let it remain on the stove on warm.

Shape the dough into 22 – 25 oval or egg shaped balls. Meanwhile heat shortening for frying. With shortening on a very low temperature, fry dough slowly until golden. Dough will automatically turn itself for cooking second side. Allow approximately 5 – 6 minutes for each batch. Remove with slotted spoon and place on paper towel to drain. While still warm to the touch, place the fried dough into the hot syrup. Allow 15 – 20 minutes to soak and soften. They will become larger as they soak up the syrup.

Serve this mouthwatering dessert after re-warming in the oven.

® Bisquick is a registered trademark of General Mills, Inc.

HEALTHY RED LENTIL SOUP

Ingredients

1 ½ cups red lentils in skins
1 cup cubed potatoes
1 cup sliced carrots
1 cup chopped tomatoes
½ tsp turmeric powder
1 ½ tsp. salt
¼ cup oil
½ tsp whole cumin
1 bay leaf
1 whole red chili, about 1" long
1 onion, chopped
½ tsp. crushed red pepper
1 tsp. grated fresh ginger root
1 tsp. sugar
1 tsp. lemon juice
1 tsp. ghee
2 tsp. Anita's bhaja masala powder
fresh cilantro leaves and chopped green chilies

Directions

Add lentils to a pot and cover with water, about 1 ½" – 2" above level of lentils. On low heat, cook soup for about 25 minutes. Add potatoes, carrots and tomatoes and cook for an additional 20 minutes. Then add turmeric powder and 1 tsp. salt. Continue to cook stirring occasionally.

In a skillet, heat oil until just beginning to smoke then add whole cumin, bay leaf and whole red chili. Fry a few seconds in oil then add chopped onion and ½ tsp. salt. Fry for 2 – 3 minutes then add crushed red pepper, ginger and sugar. Fry for a few more seconds.

Add this mixture to the pot of cooked lentils and vegetables and add a little water if necessary in order to achieve the consistency of thick soup. Keep pot uncovered on low heat. Cook for a few more minutes and then add lemon juice, ghee and Anita's bhaja masala. Garnish with cilantro and chilies. Serve as a meal with bread.

KACHURI
(Bread Stuffed with Green Peas)

Stuffing Ingredients

1 lb. fresh or frozen green peas
2 Tbsp. oil
1 tsp. grated fresh ginger root
1 tsp. sugar
2 tsp. salt
½ tsp. chili powder
1 tsp. cumin powder
½ tsp. turmeric powder
1 tsp. garam masala powder

Bread Dough Ingredients

4 cups all purpose flour
¼ cup shortening
1 tsp. salt
¼ tsp. baking soda
2 cups warm water
3 – 4 cups oil

Directions

Puree peas in a blender. In a medium frying pan, heat oil and brown ginger. Add sugar, salt and all spices for stuffing and stir well. Add pureed peas and continue stirring until all of the moisture is absorbed, about 20 minutes. The resulting mixture should be dry enough to form small balls about the size of a cherry. Cool the pureed mixture before forming the balls. It is very important that the balls are completely cooled before stuffing.

In a large mixing bowl, add flour, shortening, salt and baking soda. Slowly add water, mixing and kneading with hands to form nice soft dough (oil hands to achieve smoother dough). Divide dough into 20 – 25 plum sized balls. Flatten each ball into the palm of your hand, curving into a cup like shape. Place a prepared stuffing ball into the center of each cup and form dough around ball, pressing closed at the top. Place on a platter, cover with damp cloth and allow to rest 30 minutes. On a greased surface, roll each stuffed ball gently to a 4 inch circle, $\frac{1}{8}$ of an inch thick.

In a deep frying pan, heat oil until hot. Fry breads one at a time. When kachuri balloons on first side, turn and fry second side. This takes about 1 minute each. This bread is delicious with sweet chutney.

KHAJA

Ingredients

2 cups all purpose flour
4 cups vegetable shortening
½ cup warm water
2 Tbsp. ghee
2 Tbsp. rice flour
4 cups sugar mixed with 1 cup water

Directions

Combine 2 cups flour with 2 Tbsp shortening. Add enough warm water (approximately ½ cup) to form soft pastry dough. Divide dough into 20 – 25 plum sized balls. Roll each ball into a circle 8 inches in diameter. Combine ghee with rice flour in a mixing bowl until smooth. Drizzle rice flour mixture onto each pastry circle and spread evenly with your fingers.

Slice each prepared circle into 4 strips leaving opposite ends attached. Roll each strip as follows: roll the 1st strip down its length, around the attached outer edge and down the length of the 2nd strip. Continue in this manner with the 3rd and 4th strips. Slice the rolled pastry in half to achieve 2 thinner rolled pastries. Lay them down and flatten with the palm of your hand, then roll into thin 4" circles (you will still see the spiral pattern).

Melt remaining shortening in a deep, heavy skillet. Drop 3 – 4 circles into hot shortening. Fry slowly, patting with a spatula while they are rising. Continue to cook until lightly browned. Pastries will open like flower petals after approximately 1 minute. Remove Khaja petals from skillet with a slotted spoon and place on paper towel to drain.

On low heat, warm sugar and water mixture to form thick syrup. Glaze the top of each Khaja with the syrup.

KHEER ROLL

Kheer Ingredients

½ gallon half & half
1 cup dry milk
2 Tbsp. sugar

Directions

In heavy pot bring half & half to a boil. Stir frequently until half & half looks like thick pancake batter. Add the dry milk and sugar. Cook until it looks like soft dough. Let it cool. This will keep overnight in the refrigerator.

Batter Ingredients

1 cup fine cream of wheat
1½ cups Bisquick®
½ tsp. baking soda
2 Tbsp. sugar
1 Tbsp. ghee
1 cup half & half
½ cup buttermilk
May require ¼ cup water

Directions

Mix cream of wheat and Bisquick®, baking soda, sugar with ghee. Add half/half and buttermilk. Mix well until it resembles crepe batter. If very thick add a bit of water. Chill in refrigerator 4 - 5 hours.

Roll the kheer into 18 – 20 small, sausage-like cylinders.

Grease and heat a non-stick griddle. Pour $^1/_3$ cup of the chilled crepe-like mixture onto the griddle. Shape the mixture thin like a 4" x 6" oval crepe. When it is lightly brown place a kheer roll on the center of the crepe. With a spatula roll the crepe 3-4 times. Place them on a platter. Repeat the above steps for the rest of the kheer rolls.

Syrup Ingredients

1 cup sugar
¼ cup water
1 tsp. rose water

Directions

Boil the sugar and water until it forms thick syrup similar to pancake syrup. Add 1 tsp. rose water. Pour syrup on top of kheer rolls as desired.

® Bisquick is a registered trademark of General Mills, Inc.

KHITCHRI

Ingredients

1 cup lentils, washed
8 cups water
1 cup rice, washed
2 large potatoes, cut in quarters
2 large tomatoes, chopped if desired
2 tsp. salt
4 tsp. sugar
1 tsp. turmeric
1 head cauliflower, flowerets only
½ cup oil
1 cup peas
1 tsp. whole cumin
2 bay leaves
2 whole dried red chili peppers
1 cup chopped onion
2 tsp. grated fresh ginger root
1 Tbsp. tomato sauce
2 tsp. cumin powder
1 tsp. garam masala powder
1 tsp. chili powder
2 tsp. ghee

Directions

Boil lentils in 2 cups of water for 10 minutes. Add washed rice, 6 cups water, potatoes, tomatoes, salt, sugar and ½ tsp. of turmeric. Continue simmering until rice becomes soft. In the meantime, brown cauliflower in oil. Remove cauliflower with slotted spoon and add to the rice mixture along with peas. Then fry cumin seeds, bay leaves and chili peppers in oil that remains in pan. Add onions, grated ginger, tomato sauce, cumin powder, garam masala, remaining turmeric and chili powder. Sauté until a nice sauce is formed. Add to boiling rice mixture along with ghee. Mix well and continue simmering only long enough for the cauliflower to be just done. Mixture should resemble the consistency of bean soup.

LAMB DOPEANJA

Ingredients

4 lbs. lamb (stew meat), cut into 2" pieces
1 cup yogurt
3 tsp. salt
6 garlic cloves, grated + 1 additional tsp.
½ tsp. turmeric powder
2 tsp. chili powder
4 cups water
Whole garam masala (4 – 5 bay leaves, 6 – 8 cardamom pods, 2 2" pieces cinnamon stick, 8 – 10 peppercorns)
1 cup oil
5 – 6 medium onions, cut lengthwise into think slices
4 medium tomatoes, each cut into 4 – 6 pieces
2 Tbsp. grated fresh ginger root
4 tsp. coriander powder
2 tsp. Anita's masala
3 - 4 green chilies, sliced lengthwise
½ cup fresh cilantro leaves

Directions

Trim the lamb meat, wash and marinate in yogurt, 2 tsp. salt, 1 tsp. garlic, turmeric and ½ tsp. chili powder for about 2 hours.

In a medium pot, bring water and whole garam masala pieces to a boil. Add marinated lamb. Reduce heat to medium and cook for about 1 hour or until meat is tender, but not falling apart. Remove meat from pot and place into a bowl. Reserve 1 cup of stock including garam masala pieces and set aside.

In a medium pot, heat oil until just beginning to smoke. Add remaining garlic, ginger, onions and remaining salt. Fry until lightly browned. Add rest of powdered spices, mixing gently with the onions. Be careful not to mash the onions. Add tomatoes and cooked meat into the mixture, continuing to stir slowly for 2 minutes. Add reserved stock, lower heat and cover, cooking for an additional 4 – 5 minutes.

Dopeanja is ready for serving when the onions and tomatoes have been nicely browned in the gravy. Garnish with green chilies and fresh cilantro.

LAMB KORMA

Ingredients

½ cup plain yogurt
2 tsp. turmeric powder
4 tsp. salt
4 – 5 lbs. lamb, trimmed stew pieces
½ cup oil
1 tsp. whole cumin
A few pieces of cardamom, cloves, cinnamon stick, peppercorns and bay leaf
4 onions, finely chopped
8 cloves garlic, grated
2 tsp. grated fresh ginger root
2 tsp. sugar
1 ½ tsp. chili powder
1 Tbsp. coriander powder
2 large tomatoes, chopped or ½ cup tomato sauce
2 cups water
2 tsp. garam masala powder
¼ cup sour cream
2 tsp. ghee
2 – 3 hard boiled eggs, chopped
Fresh cilantro leaves

Directions

Mix yogurt with 1 tsp. of the turmeric and 2 tsp. of the salt. Pour over lamb pieces, stir and let marinate for 2 - 3 hours in the refrigerator. Then in a large heavy sauce pan, heat oil to point of just beginning to smoke and add all of the whole spices. Add onion, garlic and ginger. Sauté to golden brown. Then add sugar, remaining salt and all powdered spices except for the garam masala. Mix for one minute. Add tomatoes (or sauce) and continue stirring until oil separates from mixture. Add marinated lamb. Continue cooking on medium heat, stirring to prevent sticking to the pan. When the lamb begins to absorb the sauce, add water and bring to a boil. Lower heat, cover and simmer for about 20 minutes. When lamb is nicely tender but not yet falling apart, add garam masala powder, sour cream and ghee. Garnish with hard boiled eggs and cilantro. Serve with fluffy rice. Serves 6 – 8.

LAMB MEAT RIZELLA

Ingredients

3 – 4 lbs. lamb or goat cut into 2 – 3" chunks
2 tsp. salt
1 cup plain yogurt
1 cup oil
¼ cup whole garam masala
8 – 10 garlic cloves, finely chopped
4 large onions, sliced thin
2 Tbsp. grated fresh ginger root
½ tsp. ground cinnamon
1 tsp. chili powder
2 tsp. coriander powder
2 large tomatoes, cut into quarters
2 hard boiled eggs, sliced
¼ cup chopped cilantro
2 – 3 green chilies, sliced

Directions

Clean the meat and drain to remove any excess water. In a large bowl, combine 1 tsp. salt, yogurt and 2 Tbsp. of the oil. Add meat and marinate for 5 – 6 hours.

In a large heavy pot, place rest of oil and heat until just beginning to smoke. Add garam masala pieces and brown for 1 minute. Add garlic and onions cook until golden brown. Add ginger, cinnamon, chili powder and coriander powder and mix well. Add meat to the sauce and stir well to coat. Lower heat to medium. Continue to cook for 30 minutes, stirring quite often. Add remaining salt. Lower heat and cover the pot with a tight lid. Cook on low heat stirring occasionally for 45 – 60 minutes, until meat is tender. Add tomatoes 5 minutes before meat is done, mix well.

Ladle into a serving dish and garnish with sliced hard boiled eggs, cilantro and green chilies.

LAMB MOGLAI KORMA

Ingredients

½ cup milk
¼ cup raw cashews
2 tsp. poppy seeds
¾ cup butter or oil
1 lb. onions, finely chopped
8 large garlic cloves, grated
2 tsp. grated fresh ginger root
4 lbs. lean lamb, cut into 1 ½" cubes
2 tsp. coriander powder
1 tsp. cumin powder
2 tsp. salt
1 tsp. ground red pepper
1 tsp. turmeric powder
2 large tomatoes, cut into pieces
½ cup yogurt, beaten
½ cup chopped fresh cilantro leaves
1 tsp. garam masala
2 tsp. ghee

Directions

Blend milk, cashews and poppy seed in blender until smooth. Set aside.

Melt butter in a large, heavy skillet over medium-high heat. Add onions, garlic and ginger and sauté until lightly browned. Reduce heat to medium and add lamb. Sauté until browned on all sides, scraping skillet constantly to prevent sticking. Add spices, except garam masala, mixing constantly. Reduce heat to low and cook until lamb is nicely glazed, about 10 minutes.

Add tomato, yogurt and cashew-poppy seed mixture to lamb, stirring well. Cover and simmer about 20 – 25 minutes. Remove to a serving bowl and garnish with cilantro leaves. Sprinkle garam masala and ghee over dish.

LAMB PASANDA

Ingredients

1 cup oil
4 large bay leaves
8 cardamom pods
4 cups finely chopped onion
6 garlic cloves, grated
4 tsp. grated fresh ginger root
2 tsp. sugar
1 Tbsp. salt
¾ lb. lamb meat, cut into pieces
1 tsp. chili powder
2 large tomatoes, chopped
4 cups milk
2 tsp. ghee
2 tsp. garam masala powder
1 tsp. ground mace
$^1/_8$ tsp. saffron

Directions

In a heavy sauce pan, heat oil until just beginning to smoke and add bay leaves and cardamom. Then add onion, garlic, ginger, sugar and salt. Cook, stirring often, until mixture is nicely browned. This may take 15 minutes or more. Then add lamb pieces, chili powder and tomatoes. Continue to cook for 15 – 20 minutes, then add milk. Bring to a boil, cover and cook over low heat until the meat is quite tender. Remove the cover, add ghee, garam masala, mace and saffron.

This dish can be reheated before serving. Lamb pasanda is an outstanding meat dish which can be served with rice, naan or parathas.

LAMB ROGANJOSH

Ingredients

3 – 4 lbs. stewing lamb, fat removed and cut into 1 inch pieces
2 tsp. salt
1 cup yogurt
1 tsp. chili powder
½ cup butter or oil
2 tsp. sugar
6 cloves garlic, minced
2 cups grated onion
2 tsp. grated fresh ginger root or 1 tsp. ginger powder
1 Tbsp. coriander powder
½ tsp. nutmeg
½ tsp. mace
2 tsp. garam masala powder
2 fresh tomatoes, chopped
1 cup hot water
½ tsp. saffron in 1 Tbsp. hot water
1 ½ cups heavy cream

Directions

Marinate lamb in mixture of 1 tsp. salt, yogurt and chili overnight or 4 – 6 hours.

In large sauce pan heat butter, then add sugar, garlic, onions and ginger. Sauté for 5 – 7 minutes. Add all other ground spices and tomatoes. Mix well and continue sautéing until tomatoes are like a paste. Stirring constantly, add marinated lamb and marinade to mixture. Stir frequently and cook for another 15 – 20 minutes or until sauce is thick and coats meat well. Then add water and simmer, covered, for another 20 minutes or until meat is tender.

Add saffron which has been mixed with 1 Tbsp. of hot water (this releases the color). Pour heavy cream into mixture, combine well.

Serve this delicious, rich maglai dish with rice and Indian bread.

LAMB VINDALOO

Ingredients

2 cups plain yogurt
1 Tbsp. salt
2 Tbsp. turmeric powder
3 – 4 lbs. lamb meat, fat removed, cut into small cubes
1 cup oil
1 tsp. cumin
1 tsp. red mustard seeds
4 onions, finely chopped
8 – 10 garlic cloves, grated
2 Tbsp. grated fresh ginger root
4 tsp. coriander powder
2 tsp. chili powder
2 cups tomato sauce or fresh chopped tomatoes
2 cups sour cream
2 Tbsp. blended mustard paste (1/4 cup red mustard seeds soaked in hot water for 1 hour and processed in a blender until a paste is formed)
1 tsp. garam masala powder
2 – 3 green chilies, chopped
1 cup cilantro leaves

Directions

In a large bowl, combine yogurt, 1 tsp salt and 1 tsp. turmeric powder. Add meat and marinate over night in the refrigerator.

In a heavy sauce pan heat oil, cumin, red mustard and sugar. When sugar becomes brown in the oil, add chopped onions, garlic and ginger. Stir the mixture constantly until it is dark brown. Add coriander, chili powder, tomato sauce, remaining turmeric and salt.

Stir the spices until well mixed.

Add marinated lamb and coat with sauce mixture. When liquid begins to bleed from meat, lower heat, cover and let simmer for 30 minutes. Occasionally stir the mixture so that it does not stick to the bottom of the pan. When lamb is tender, add the sour cream, mustard paste, garam masala, green chilies and coriander leaves. Continue to stir until the sauce becomes a dry paste.

This dish is mouthwatering, very spicy and hot. Serve with plain rice or chapati. To soothe the palate, serve plain raita with this dish. Serves 6 – 8.

LUCHI

Ingredients

1 cup all purpose flour
1 cup whole wheat flour
1 Tbsp. shortening
½ tsp. sugar
½ tsp. salt
1 cup warm water
2 cups oil

Directions

Combine flour, shortening, sugar and salt. Add water slowly to make cohesive dough. Knead well with hands until smooth. Cover with a damp cloth and let stand at room temperature for 30 minutes.

Shape dough into 20 – 25 walnut sized balls. Roll out into 4" circles, $^1/_8$" thick. In a deep frying pan, heat oil until hot. Put a pinch of dough in hot oil to test temperature. Dough should rise immediately. Fry one at a time. When the luchi balloons on one side, turn to the other. This should take less than a minute per side. Remove with a slotted spoon and drain on paper towel. Serve immediately.

MALPOA

Ingredients

2 cups cream of wheat
1 cup all purpose flour
2 cups powdered milk
¼ cup butter, melted
2 tsp. fennel seeds
½ tsp. black pepper
½ tsp. salt
½ cup raisins
1 cup ricotta cheese
½ tsp. baking soda
½ gallon of half & half and 1 qt. of milk, boiled and thickened
to the consistency of cream
½ cup warm water
4 cups shortening

Syrup Ingredients

4 cups sugar
6 cups water

Directions

Add first 10 ingredients to a bowl and mix well. Stir in
thickened half & half/milk and water. The mixture should look like
pancake batter. Set aside for 2 hours at room temperature.

Heat shortening in a large skillet. Fry 2 Tbsp. of batter in
shortening at a time. Batter should spread looking like a 4 inch
pancake. Fry malpoa until golden brown, removing with a spatula
to a paper towel to drain. Continue with remaining batter.

In the meantime, bring sugar and water to a boil for 2 – 3 minutes in a shallow pan for syrup. Add a few malpoas at a time to hot syrup. Remove after 3 – 4 minutes and place on a platter. If syrup begins to thicken at any time, thin by warming. May be served hot or cold.

MANGO CHUTNEY

Ingredients

2 large green mangos
1 tsp. salt
½ cup water
3 cups sugar
1 ½ cups raisins
2 tsp. slivered fresh ginger root
1 Tbsp. oil
½ tsp. red mustard seeds
1 small green chili, chopped
2 tsp. chutney masala powder

Directions

Peel mango and cut into chunks, discarding seed. Place mango, salt and water into a sauce pan and boil until mango is tender. Add sugar, raisins and ginger and cook on medium heat until mangos have the consistency of a chunky sauce.

Heat oil in a small frying pan until just beginning to smoke, add mustard seeds and green chili. When seeds begin to jump in pan, pour into mango sauce. Reduce heat and add chutney masala to mixture and simmer for 1 minute.

Chutney is best made 1 day ahead and served chilled.

MANGO KULFI

Ingredients

½ gallon half & half
2 cups sugar
8 oz. container of ricotta cheese
4 mangos, pureed
1 Tbsp. corn starch mixed with ¼ cup water

Directions

Bring half & half to a boil and continue to cook until reduced by half. Add sugar, cheese and corn starch mixture. Mixture will become thick custard like. Cool, add mango puree, pour into a bowl and place in freezer. When semi-solid, put into a blender and blend until smooth and creamy. Refreeze in popsicle molds or a 9 x 13 inch pan to be cut into 2 inch squares. When kulfi is completely solid, serve on a dessert plate.

MASOOR DHAL
(Red Lentils)

Ingredients

1 ½ cups red lentils
½ tsp turmeric powder
1 ½ tsp. salt
¼ cup oil
½ tsp whole cumin
1 bay leaf
1 whole red chili, about 1" long
1 onion, chopped
1 tsp. cumin powder
½ tsp. crushed red pepper
1 tsp. grated fresh ginger root
1 tsp. sugar
1 tsp. ghee
fresh cilantro leaves and chopped green chilies

Directions

Add lentils to a pot and cover with water, about 1 ½" – 2" above level of lentils. On low heat, cook for about 30 minutes or until lentils can be mashed with a spoon. Then add turmeric powder and 1 tsp. salt. Continue to cook, stirring occasionally, uncovered until a creamy paste is formed.

In a skillet, heat oil until just beginning to smoke then add whole cumin, bay leaf and whole red chili. Fry a few seconds in oil then add chopped onion and ½ tsp. salt. Fry for 2 – 3 minutes then add cumin powder, crushed red pepper, ginger and sugar. Fry for a few more seconds.

Add this mixture to the pot of cooked lentils and add a little water if necessary in order to achieve the consistency of thick soup. Keep pot uncovered on low heat. Cook for a few more minutes and then add ghee. Garnish with cilantro and chilies. Serve over plain rice.

MATAR PANEER
(Peas)

Paneer Ingredients

1 gallon 2% milk
1 cup lemon juice

Directions

In large pan, bring milk to a rapid boil. Add lemon juice. Milk will separate into fresh cheese with a light lemon color. Line a large strainer with cheese cloth and pour cheese mixture into it. Press to remove all liquid so cheese becomes dry. On a large plate, flatten cheese into a ¾ inch high block. Place a heavy weight over the block and continue to squeeze out any remaining liquid.

Cut cheese block into ½ inch squares and set aside.

Matar Paneer Ingredients

½ cup oil
1 tsp. of whole cumin
Few pieces each of bay leaves, cardamom and cinnamon stick
2 Tbsp. chopped fresh ginger root
2 tsp. salt
2 tsp. sugar
1 tsp. turmeric powder
1 tsp. chili powder
2 tsp. Anita's bhaja masala powder
1 tsp. coriander powder
2 medium sized, ripe tomatoes, finely chopped or 1 cup crushed tomato sauce

½ cup yogurt
1 ½ lb. frozen baby peas
1 cup water
½ tsp. ground cinnamon
1 tsp. ghee
½ cup chopped fresh cilantro leaves
Few pieces of green chilly
½ cup cream

Directions

In a deep frying pan, heat oil until just beginning to smoke. Add cheese pieces a few at a time and fry until lightly browned. Remove to a platter and set aside.

Add whole cumin, bay leaves, cardamom and cinnamon stick pieces to remaining oil and stir for a few seconds. Then add chopped ginger, salt, sugar, turmeric, chili powder, Anita's bhaja masala powder, coriander powder, tomatoes and yogurt. Stir until mixture becomes a paste. Then add peas, stir and continue to cook for a few minutes. Add water and cheese pieces. On medium heat, cook for 2 – 3 minutes more.

Add ground cinnamon, ghee and cream. Stir then pour onto a platter. Spread cilantro and chili pieces over dish. Serves 8 – 10 with rice or naan.

MIXED FRUIT CHUTNEY

Ingredients

2 Tbsp. oil
1 tsp. dry red mustard
1 Tbsp. finely chopped fresh ginger root
½ tsp. turmeric powder
2 lbs. chopped fresh tomatoes
2 tsp. salt
1 16 oz. can pineapple
1 16 oz. can peaches
1 cup prunes
1 cup dates
1 cup raisins
2 cups sugar
1 cup water
2 tsp. chutney masala powder
1 Tbsp. lime juice

Directions

Heat oil in a sauce pan then fry mustard for 1 – 2 minutes. Add ginger, turmeric, tomatoes and salt. Fry until the tomatoes are like paste. Add all other fruit, sugar and water. Bring to a boil and cook on low heat for 30 – 40 minutes. When quite thick, remove from heat. Add chutney masala and lime juice. Serve cold; can be refrigerated for 2 – 3 weeks.

MOGHULI KABAB

Ingredients

½ tsp. saffron
2 Tbsp. water
3 – 4 lbs. ground lamb or turkey
2 cups grated onion
4 – 6 cloves garlic, grated
2 tsp. grated fresh ginger root
½ cup yogurt
½ cup graham flour (chick pea flour)
2 Tbsp. oil
1 tsp. cumin powder
1 tsp coriander powder
1 tsp. chili powder or 2 tsp. of freshly grated green chili pepper
¼ cup chopped fresh cilantro
1 tsp. garam masala powder

Directions

In a small skillet, lightly crisp saffron (about 30 seconds). Add water and set aside.

Combine all remaining ingredients in a large mixing bowl. Mix well with hands to give a smooth texture. Add saffron liquid and mix well. Let meat mixture stand at room temperature for 45 minutes. Shape 3 inch kabobs on skewers – should fit 3 to 4 kabobs per skewer. On a grill, cook 15 – 20 minutes, rotating evenly. Do not cook too fast and keep kabobs about 2 inches from flame.

Moghuli Kabab is delicious as hors d'oeuvres or a main dish served with rice and chutney.

MOGLAI CHICKEN CURRY
(with Blended Poppy Seeds and Coconut)

Ingredients

½ cup oil
Whole garam masala (4 pieces of bay leaf, 4 cardamom pods, 4 pieces cinnamon stick, 4 whole cloves and 4 peppercorns)
4 onions, chopped
3 garlic cloves, grated
2 tsp. grated fresh ginger root
2 tsp. sugar
1 tsp. salt
2 fresh tomatoes, cut into pieces or 1 cup crushed tomato sauce
1 tsp. ground nutmeg
1 tsp. chili powder
3 tsp. garam masala powder
4 lbs. chicken legs and thighs, skinned
½ cup white poppy seeds, soaked in water
1 cup grated fresh coconut
½ tsp. ghee

Directions

Heat oil in a large skillet until just beginning to smoke, then add whole garam masala spices, onions, garlic and ginger and fry until lightly browned. Add sugar, salt and tomatoes and mix well. Add nutmeg, chili powder and 2 tsp. garam masala powder and cook for about 5 minutes or until mixture becomes a rich paste. Add chicken pieces and stir well, cooking for 8 – 10 more minutes or until juice begins to run from the meat.

Drain water from the poppy seeds and place in a blender with a few tsp. of water and coconut. Blend well, then add poppy seed mixture to chicken and stir. Cover chicken and cook until meat is tender. Add remaining garam masala powder and ghee then heat for 2 more minutes.

NAAN BREAD

Ingredients

8 cups all purpose flour (can substitute 4 of the cups with whole wheat flour)
1 tsp. salt
1 tsp. sugar
1 tsp. rapid-rise yeast combined with ½ cup warm water
$^2/_3$ cup oil (reserve a small amount for later mixing)
2 cups plain yogurt mixed with 2 cups water and heated on stove until hot
Additional flour for rolling
Ghee

Directions

With hands, mix together dry ingredients and oil in large mixing bowl. Add yogurt liquid to dry mixture a small amount at a time until well combined and doughy. When fully mixed add remaining oil to make smooth (the dough should feel a bit stickier than regular bread dough). Cover with damp dish towel and let dough rise at least 2 hours (punch down once).

Form dough into 20 – 25 racquetball sized balls. Spread flour on counter. Roll each ball (with rolling pin) into $^1/_8$ inch thick, 8 inch diameter pancakes. Cook on flat griddle or slope-sided chapati griddle until lightly browned. Place each piece on foil under broiler and continue cooking until naan puffs up, about 20 seconds per side. After each naan finishes cooking, coat both sides with ghee.

Naan can be frozen and then reheated in oven wrapped in foil.

NURGISH KUFTA

Ingredients

3 – 4 lbs. ground turkey or chicken
6 medium onions, finely chopped
6 garlic cloves, grated
3 tsp. grated fresh ginger root
4 tsp. salt
2 tsp. turmeric powder
2 tsp. chili powder
2 eggs
1½ cups oil
½ tsp. softened butter
2 tsp. coriander powder
1 tsp. ground cinnamon
4 tomatoes, finely chopped
2 tsp. sugar
1 cup yogurt
1 Tbsp. garam masala powder
1 cup water

Directions

In a large bowl, combine ground meat, $^1/_3$ of the onion, ½ of the garlic, 1 tsp. grated ginger, 2 tsp. salt, 1 tsp. turmeric, 1 tsp. chili powder and eggs. Mix well and form into small egg shaped balls.

Heat 1 cup of the oil in a small frying pan. Brown meat balls a few at a time then place in a baking dish.

In a small pan, heat remaining oil and butter. Add remaining onions, garlic and ginger and fry until lightly browned. Add remaining spices except garam masala. Add tomatoes, sugar and yogurt continuing to cook for 5 – 6 minutes over low heat while stirring frequently. Add garam masala and water to mixture before pouring over the meat balls. Cover dish with foil and bake at 350° for 25 – 30 minutes.

This delicious dish can be served with rice or naan bread.

PALAK PANEER
(Spinach Paneer)

Ingredients

1 gallon milk
1 cup lemon juice
½ cup oil
1 tsp. whole cumin
2 large onions, chopped
1 tsp. grated fresh ginger root
1 tsp. sugar
4 tsp. salt
2 large tomatoes
½ cup plain yogurt
1 tsp. chili powder
1 tsp. cumin powder
2 tsp. turmeric powder
2 packages fresh spinach, finely chopped in blender
1 cup water
2 tsp. ghee
2 tsp. garam masala powder

Directions

In large pan, bring milk to a rapid boil. Add lemon juice. Milk will separate into fresh cheese with a light lemon color. Line a large strainer with cheese cloth and pour cheese mixture into it. Press to remove all liquid so cheese becomes dry. On a large plate, flatten cheese into a 1 inch high block. Cut cheese into squares and keep dry.

Add oil to a frying pan and heat. Add pieces of cheese and fry until golden brown. Set aside.

Pour remaining oil into a clean, medium sized pan and heat until just beginning to smoke. Then, add cumin, onion, ginger, sugar and salt. Fry until onion browns. Add tomatoes, yogurt, chili powder, cumin powder and turmeric powder. Cook while mixing until oil separates from sauce. Add spinach and mix well. Add water and cook for 5 minutes. Next, add cheese pieces, ghee and garam masala. Cover and simmer for 3 – 4 more minutes. Serve this dish with rice or Naan.

PANEER KUFTA

Paneer Ingredients

1 gallon 2% milk
1 cup lemon juice

Directions

In large pan, bring milk to a rapid boil. Add lemon juice. Milk will separate into fresh cheese with a light lemon color. Line a large strainer with cheese cloth and pour cheese mixture into it. Press to remove all liquid so cheese becomes dry. On a large plate, flatten cheese into a 1 inch high block.

Paneer Kufta Ingredients

2 Tbsp. all purpose flour
2 tsp. salt
2 tsp. sugar
1 tsp. turmeric powder
1 tsp. chili powder
2 tsp. Anita's bhaja masala powder
1 cup oil
1 tsp. of whole cumin
Few pieces each of bay leaves, cardamom and cinnamon stick
4 medium sized potatoes, peeled and cut into 1" – 1 ½" pieces
2 Tbsp. chopped fresh ginger root
2 medium sized, ripe tomatoes, finely chopped or 1 cup crushed tomato sauce
2 cups water
½ tsp. ground cinnamon
1 Tbsp. ghee

Directions

Crumble prepared paneer and place into a mixing bowl. Add flour, 1 tsp. salt, 1 tsp. sugar, ½ tsp. turmeric, ½ tsp. chili powder and 1 tsp. Anita's bhaja masala. Mix and knead well to make dough. Divide into 25 pieces and form into balls.

In a deep frying pan, heat oil until just beginning to smoke. Add about 10 balls of dough at a time and fry until golden brown. Remove to a platter.

Add whole cumin, bay leaves, cardamom and cinnamon stick pieces to remaining oil and stir for a few seconds. Then add potato and lightly brown. Add chopped ginger, remaining salt, sugar, turmeric, chili powder and Anita's bhaja masala powder. Add tomatoes, continuing to stir until sauce becomes a smooth paste. Then add water and boil until potatoes are almost thoroughly cooked.

Add fried paneer balls and cook for 1 minute; until soft and spongy. Add ground cinnamon and ghee. Stir then remove to a platter. Serves 8 – 10 with bread or rice.

PANEER PILLAU
(with Cheese Pieces)

Paneer Ingredients

½ gallon whole milk
½ cup concentrated lemon juice
2 – 3 cups ice
1 Tbsp. ghee

Directions

Pour milk into a large bowl and microwave for 30 minutes, bringing it just to a boil. Remove milk from the microwave and add lemon juice and lightly stir. Paneer will form and a light green liquid will separate from it. Add ice to the bowl and allow mixture to stand for 5 minutes.

In a large enough strainer, line with cheese cloth and pour contents of bowl through. Squeeze the paneer tightly to eliminate all liquid. Form into a ball wrapped in the cheese cloth. Flatten ball to ½" thickness, rest on a plate, weight the top and refrigerate overnight. When ready to cook pillau, cut the paneer into ½" cubes.

In a small frying pan, heat ghee and fry paneer cubes until golden brown and set aside.

Pillau Ingredients

2 cups Basmati rice
1 cup ghee
½ cup whole garam masala (4 – 5 bay leaves, 8 – 10

cardamom pods, a few pieces cinnamon stick, 8 – 10 black peppercorns)
½ cup sliced almonds
4 tsp. sugar
2 tsp. salt
½ cup raisins
¼ tsp. saffron
¼ tsp. chili powder
1 Tbsp. grated fresh ginger root
25 pieces ½" paneer cubes
¼ cup heavy cream
4 cups water

Directions

Wash rice and drain on paper towel for an hour.

In a 4 Qt. pot, heat ghee until it begins to smoke lightly. Add all whole garam masala pieces and almonds, slowly frying until lightly browned. Add sugar, salt, raisins, saffron, chili powder and ginger, mixing well. Add the drained rice into ghee mixture and stir well to mix thoroughly. Rice should be well coated by ghee mixture. Add paneer pieces and stir. Add heavy cream and enough of the 4 cups of water to cover the rice and paneer. Bring to a boil for 10 minutes or until water is almost absorbed. Cover tightly and cook rice for another 10 minutes on very low heat just until the rice is fluffy.

The dish is ready for serving.

PARAKEE
(Pastry Stuffed with Coconut)

Ingredients

2 fresh coconuts, peeled and grated
3 cups sugar
½ cup milk
2 cups all purpose flour
¼ tsp. baking soda
$^1/_8$ tsp. salt
2 Tbsp. butter
½ - 1 cup warm water
4 cups shortening
4 cups sugar mixed with 1 cup water for syrup

Directions

Combine grated coconut, sugar and milk in a heavy sauce pan. Cook for 25 minutes or until mixture reaches a consistency where a soft ball may be formed.

Combine flour, baking soda, salt and butter and mix well by hand. Slowly add ½ - 1 cup warm water to form smooth, soft dough; using only as much water as needed. Knead well with hands until dough texture is very soft and smooth. Form into walnut sized balls. Roll each ball into a 3 x 4 inch oval shape approximately $^1/_8$ inch thick.

Place 1 Tbsp. of coconut filling on one end of each oval pastry. Fold in half and secure edges by pinching closed. Hold on palm of one hand while fluting pastry edges with the other. This creates a pretty ruffled edge.

Heat shortening in a deep frying pan and fry 4 – 5 pastries at a time. Fry slowly until golden and crispy. Remove pastries with a slotted spoon to a paper towel to drain. While frying, heat sugar and water mixture until thick syrup forms. Dip each cooked pastry into syrup and remove to a tray quickly. A glaze will form on the pastry as soon as the syrup has dried. Do not cover until glaze has completely dried.

PARATHAS

Ingredients

1 lb. whole wheat flour
1 lb. all purpose flour
1 ½ tsp. salt
1 ½ tsp. sugar
¼ cup butter, melted
2 cups warm water
1 cup oil

Directions

Mix flour, salt, sugar and melted butter in a large bowl with hands. Add water as necessary to make dough semi firm and cleanly pulls away from sides of bowl. Dough shouldn't be too hard or too soft.

Grease hands to prevent sticking and knead dough until smooth. Dampen hands with water as you work in order to keep dough soft. Cover dough with a damp cloth and let rest for 15 – 20 minutes. Divide dough into 20 – 25 balls. Sprinkle surface with flour as needed. Roll to $\frac{1}{8}$ inch thick rounds and fold in half. Folding in half again, you should be left with a triangle. Continue this process with all balls of dough.

Fry 2 – 3 triangles at a time on an un-greased griddle or skillet. Sprinkle with oil, frequently turning until lightly browned.

Makes 20 – 25 parathas. Serve hot with chutney or lamb korma. Can be made 1 day ahead, reheating in a 350° oven for 1 – 2 minutes just before serving.

Paratha

PARATHA ROLLS WITH MEAT

Ingredients

2 lbs. lamb or pork, cut into small pieces
4 ½ tsp. salt
2 Tbsp. oil
2 large onions, finely chopped
4 garlic cloves
2 tsp. grated fresh ginger root
½ tsp. chili powder
1 tsp. coriander powder
2 ½ tsp. sugar
1 cup yogurt
2 tsp. garam masala powder
2 lbs. all purpose white flour (not whole wheat)
½ cup butter, melted
2 cups warm water
Ghee
2 fresh, firm tomatoes, cut into pieces
1 small onion, chopped
1 large firm green pepper, chopped

Directions

In a large pot, place meat, 1 tsp. salt and enough water to cover meat and boil until tender. Drain.

Heat oil in a heavy skillet and fry onions, garlic and ginger until lightly browned. Add chili powder, coriander powder, 2 tsp. salt, 1 tsp. sugar and yogurt. Add meat and cook for 8 – 10 minutes or until yogurt sauce has absorbed into meat. Add garam masala powder.

Make paratha dough by combining flour, 1 ½ tsp. salt, 1 ½ tsp. sugar and melted butter. Mix by hand until smooth. Add 2 cups warm water as necessary to make dough semi firm and comes clean from sides of bowl (dough shouldn't be too hard or too soft). Form dough into large egg sized balls. Roll into very thin rounds.

Fry parathas on ungreased griddle or skillet until lightly browned. Fry 2 – 3 at a time, sprinkle with ghee and turn often (use about 1 tsp. ghee per paratha). Stack fried parathas on top of each other to keep soft. If they are fried individually and not stacked they will dry out.

Combine tomatoes, small onion and green pepper into a small bowl. Reheat meat mixture and add the above vegetables. Place about 2 -3 Tbsp. of mixture as a stripe down the middle of each paratha. Fold over one side and roll up. Parathas can be reheated in oven covered with foil to keep from drying out. Serve on a tray.

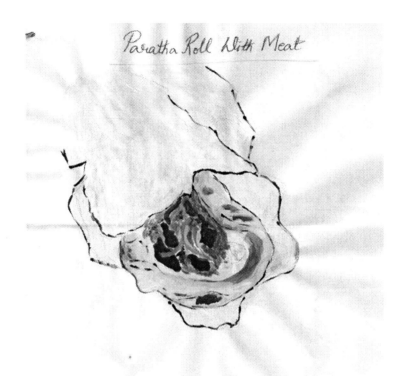

Paratha Roll With Meat

PAYESH
(Rice Pudding)

Ingredients

½ cup Basmati rice
1 tsp. ghee
3 qt. milk
1 qt. half & half
1 ½ cups sugar
½ cup chopped almonds
½ tsp. cardamom powder

Directions

Wash rice and place on paper towel to dry.

In a large, shallow saucepan heat ghee and brown the rice. Then pour milk and half & half in the pan, bring to a boil and cook over medium-low heat while stirring frequently. Watch carefully and do not allow milk to boil over or stick to bottom of pan. Continue to cook until reaching the consistency of heavy cream, about 2 hours. Stir in sugar and almonds and cook for an additional 4 – 5 minutes, stirring constantly. Serve warm or chilled and sprinkle with ground cardamom.

PINEAPPLE CHUTNEY

Ingredients

1 16 oz. can pineapple chunks with juice
2 cups sugar
1 tsp. salt
1 tsp. fresh ginger root, cut into small pieces
½ cup raisins
1 Tbsp. corn starch
½ cup water
2 Tbsp. oil
1 tsp. red mustard seeds
1 tsp. chutney masala powder

Directions

Place pineapple and its juice, sugar, salt, ginger and raisins in a saucepan and bring to a boil. Simmer 10 minutes. Mix cornstarch with water. Add to boiling mixture and bring to a second boil. Simmer for 2 more minutes.

Heat oil in small saucepan until just beginning to smoke, add mustard seeds and fry until they begin to jump. Add seed mixture to pineapple mixture along with chutney masala and cool.

PLAIN RICE

Ingredients

2 cups washed plain basmati rice
3 ½ cups water

Directions

Bring water and rice to a boil in a sauce pan. Lower heat to medium and continue to cook for approximately 15 minutes checking regularly for water absorption. When only a small amount of water is left, reduce heat to low and cover tightly. Continue to cook for an additional 5 – 6 minutes or until dry and fluffy.

This procedure can also be done in the microwave on high. Using a microwave proof bowl, cook for 20 minutes (uncovered). Remove from microwave and cover.

PLUM CHUTNEY

Ingredients

2 lb. ripe plums
2 cups sugar
1 tsp. salt
½ cup raisins
1 Tbsp. chopped fresh ginger root
¼ tsp. turmeric powder
½ cup water
2 Tbsp. oil
1 tsp. whole red mustard seeds
½ tsp. crushed red chili pepper
1 Tbsp. chutney masala

Directions

Wash plums and split into halves discarding pits.

To a medium pan, add plums, sugar, salt, raisins, ginger, turmeric and water. On high, bring to a boil, then lower heat to simmer until plums can be mashed into a sauce.

In a small frying pan, heat oil to the point of just beginning to smoke. Add mustard seed. As seeds begin to spatter in pan, add crushed chili and then pour mixture onto cooked plums. Turn off heat, mix well and then sprinkle with chutney masala.

Chutney can be preserved as such in a jar for 1 – 2 months if refrigerated. Plum chutney goes very well with many Indian meals and/or breads.

POTATO, CAULIFLOWER AND PEAS TARKAREE

Ingredients

½ cup oil
1 large head cauliflower, cut in pieces
1 Tbsp. salt
1 tsp. whole cumin
4 large potatoes, cut into 1" cubes
1 large onion, chopped
2 tsp. turmeric
1 tsp chili powder
1 tsp. cumin powder
1 Tbsp. grated fresh ginger root
2 medium tomatoes, chopped or ½ cup tomato sauce
1 16 oz. package fresh or frozen peas
1 cup water
2 fresh hot green chilies, cut into quarters
fresh cilantro leaves

Directions

In a large skillet heat oil. Add cauliflower and 1 tsp. salt and sauté until lightly browned. Remove this mixture into a separate bowl. Add whole cumin to remaining oil in skillet and fry for 30 seconds. Add potato and onion and fry until lightly browned. Add remaining spices along with ginger, salt and tomatoes. Cook and stir until spices are well mixed. Add peas, chilies and sautéed cauliflower and water. Cover the skillet with heat on low until vegetables are cooked. Garnish with fresh cilantro leaves.

This vegetarian dish can be served with ghee bhath or naan bread.

RASH MALAI

Ingredients

1 gallon milk
1 cup lemon juice
8 cups water and 1 cup ice
2 tsp. cream of wheat (or plain flour) and ½ tsp. ghee, mixed
well
3 cups sugar
2 qt. half & half (or whole milk)
2 Tbsp. rose water or ½ tsp. ground cardamom (or any desired
flavoring)

Directions

Bring milk to a rapid boil in a large sauce pan, and then add lemon juice. Milk will separate into a white cheese and water will be light lemon colored. Line a large strainer with cheese cloth and strain cheese. Press as much liquid from cheese as possible, and then allow to drain for at least 1 hour. Cheese should be dry. Mix cream of wheat mixture into cheese and knead well. Once cheese is smooth and creamy, divide and form into 20 – 25 walnut sized balls.

Bring 4 cups of water and 2 cups sugar to a boil. Add cheese balls to boiling syrup, rolling often. Combine ice into remaining water and sprinkle ice water on top of boiling pot 4 – 5 times for 20 minutes. Once they have doubled in size, lower heat and cook for 20 minutes.

While cheese cooks, bring half & half to a boil in a medium sized pan. Lower heat, but continue to boil until thickened and reduced by half. Add 1 cup sugar and cheese balls into mixture.

Cool, then add flavoring.

This delicious dessert is from Bengal.

RHUBARB CHUTNEY

Ingredients

2 lb. reddened rhubarb, cut into 1" pieces
2 cups sugar
1 tsp. salt
½ cup golden raisins
1 Tbsp. finely chopped fresh ginger root
½ cup water
2 Tbsp. oil
1 tsp. whole red mustard seeds
2 tsp. chutney masala

Directions

Combine 1st 6 ingredients in a medium size pot and bring to a boil on medium heat. Lower heat to simmer for 20 – 25 minutes or until rhubarb is nicely stewed and mixture has thickened.

In a small frying pan, heat oil to the point of just beginning to smoke. Add mustard seeds and fry until seeds begin to jump. Remove from heat and add to rhubarb mixture. Add chutney masala and combine well. Serve warm or cooled.

RICE PILLAU

Ingredients

½ cup ghee
A few cardamom pods
A few pieces of cinnamon stick
A few bay leaves
1 cup chopped onion
1 tsp. sugar
2 tsp. salt
3 cups basmati rice, rinsed
5 cups water
$^1/_8$ tsp. saffron
1 tsp. garam masala powder

Directions

Pour ghee and the whole pieces of spice into a 4 qt. saucepan. Fry spices for 30 seconds. Add onion, sugar and salt. Continue to fry until lightly browned. Add rice and stir until mixture is well coated. Add water and allow rice to boil for a couple of minutes. Add saffron and garam masala powder. Cover saucepan, lower heat and allow rice to simmer for 20 minutes until water is absorbed and rice is fluffy.

This rice can be served with any meat and/or vegetable dishes.

ROASTED MUGE DHAL
(Bhaja Muge Dhal with Potato and Cauliflower)

Ingredients

1 ½ cups plain muge dhal
3 cups water
2 tsp. salt
½ cup oil
Foran (1 tsp. whole cumin, 2 – 3 pieces bay leaves and 2 – 3 pieces dry red chili pepper)
1 large potato, cut into small pieces
½ cauliflower head, broken into 1" pieces
¼ tsp. turmeric powder
1 tsp. chili powder
2 tsp. Anita's bhaja masala powder
1 Tbsp. ginger paste
1 large tomato, cut into 4 pieces
2 tsp. sugar
½ cup fresh peas
1 tsp. ghee
¼ cup fresh cilantro leaves
2 green chilies, sliced

Directions

Roast muge dhal in a frying pan on medium heat. Continuously stir to ensure that dhal only lightly browns, although a few grains may become dark in the process. Wash roasted muge dhal then add to a medium sized pot with water and 1 tsp. salt. Bring to a rolling boil, then lower heat and simmer until the dhal can be mashed with a spoon. Cover the pot and set aside.

In a medium sized frying pan, heat the oil until just beginning

150

to smoke and add foran. Then add potatoes, cauliflower pieces and 1 tsp salt. Stir until lightly browned. Move fried pieces to one side to make room for spices. Add turmeric, chili powder, Anita's bhaja masala, ginger paste, tomato pieces, sugar and fresh peas and cook for 2 minutes. Mix together everything in pan. At this point ½ cup of water mixed into spices may be necessary to remove mixture from pan.

Add spice mixture to prepared dhal. Mix well and boil for about 2 minutes. Remove cauliflower dhal to a soup tureen and garnish with ghee, cilantro leaves and green chilies. Serve with luchis and/or parathas on the side. Serves 8 – 10.

ROSE WATER KULFI

Ingredients

½ gallon half & half
2 cups sugar
8 oz. container of ricotta cheese
1 tsp. rose water
1 Tbsp. corn starch mixed with ¼ cup water

Directions

Bring half & half to a boil and continue to cook until reduced by half. Add sugar, cheese and corn starch mixture. Mixture will become thick custard like. Cool, add rose water, pour into a bowl and place in freezer. When semi-solid, put into a blender and blend until smooth and creamy. Refreeze in popsicle molds or a 9 x 13 inch pan to be cut into 2 inch squares. When kulpi is completely solid, serve on a dessert plate.

ROYAL MOGHULI LAMB ROAST
(with Chiffon Rice)

Ingredients

Leg of lamb (preferably boned)
4 medium onions, 1 grated and 3 sliced
3 tsp. salt
2 tsp. grated fresh ginger
1 tsp. grated garlic
2 Tbsp. lemon juice
1 ½ cups ghee
2 tsp. sugar
1 tsp. chili powder
1 cup yogurt, beaten
2 cups rice
8 cups water
½ cup slivered almonds
½ cup cashews
½ cup fresh coconut pieces
½ cup pistachios
¼ cup whole pieces of garam masala (cardamom, cinnamon, cloves, peppercorn and bay leaves)
½ tsp. saffron
1 tsp. garam masala powder
1 cup heavy cream
2 fresh green chilies, chopped
½ cup chopped fresh cilantro leaves

Directions

Wash and dry lamb, then set aside in a baking dish. Make multiple slits all over lamb surface. Mix grated onion with 1 tsp. of salt, 1 tsp. of grated ginger, all of the garlic and lemon juice. Rub

153

the mixture over pierced lamb surface and let stand for a couple of hours.

In a small pan, combine ½ cup of ghee with 1 tsp. sugar, chili powder, 1 tsp. of grated ginger and yogurt. Cook slowly until a smooth cream sauce results, about 5 – 6 minutes. Pour $^2/_3$ of this sauce over the lamb. Cover with foil and cook in a 350° oven for 1 hour. Remove from oven and baste with remaining sauce and pan drippings. Return to oven for another 30 – 45 minutes.

In the meantime, wash rice. Then in a large saucepan, cook rice in 8 cups of water just until tender (do not over cook). Drain and dry rice, then set aside.

In a frying pan, heat remaining ghee. Fry the almonds, then the cashews, then the coconut, and then the pistachios; remove one item with a slotted spoon before adding the next keeping each ingredient separated. Set these aside. Fry sliced onions until golden brown, remove from pan with slotted spoon. In the same pan brown the whole garam masala ingredients. Add remaining sugar, salt, ginger, saffron and garam masala powder. Slowly add cream to make a sauce for the rice.

Remove lamb from oven and place in a large Corning roaster (or similar baking dish). Pour drippings from pan back over the lamb and spread cooked rice around it. Pour rice sauce evenly over rice. Then spread fried ingredients attractively over rice and lamb. Cover with foil and bake another 30 minutes at same temperature. Remove from oven and garnish with chilies and cilantro.

This delicious Indian recipe will serve 8 - 10 and is indeed a royal dish!

SAMBAR DHAL

Ingredients

1 cup red lentils
1 cup yellow split peas
4 cups water
2 tsp. salt
2 large fresh tomatoes, chopped
½ tsp. turmeric powder
1 large green mango, cut up or 3 stalks rhubarb, cut into ½"
pieces
½ cup oil
1 Tbsp. red mustard seeds
2 tsp. sambar masala powder
2 tsp. grated fresh ginger root
2 tsp. sugar
½ tsp. crushed red pepper
4 – 6 cups fresh vegetable, chopped– any combination of:
    Carrots
    Cauliflower
    Eggplant
    Green beans
    Onion
    Potatoes
    Squash
2 tsp. ghee
Fresh cilantro leaves
2 – 3 chilies, sliced

Directions

Boil lentils and peas in a large sauce pan in 4 cups of water
until very soft. Add salt, tomatoes and turmeric. Mixture will look

like a thick soup, then add mango or rhubarb and continue simmering.

In the meantime, heat oil in a frying pan until just beginning to smoke then add mustard seeds. When seeds begin to pop, stir in sambar masala, grated ginger, sugar, crushed red pepper and vegetables. Brown vegetables then add lentil/pea mixture. Cook until vegetables are tender. Add ghee and garnish with fresh cilantro and chilies.

SAMOSAS

Filling Ingredients

½ cup oil
1 tsp. whole cumin
2 medium onions, chopped
6 potatoes, peeled and cubed
1 small head of cauliflower, cut into bite sized pieces
1 package frozen peas
1 tsp. turmeric powder
2 tsp. salt
1 tsp. crushed red pepper
1 tsp. grated fresh ginger root
1 tsp. sugar
2 tsp. garam masala powder

Directions

Heat oil in a frying pan, add cumin seed and fry one minute. Add onion and fry until golden brown. Add all other ingredients and stir well. Cover and reduce heat, stirring occasionally until vegetables are fully cooked. Finally add garam masala powder.

Dough Ingredients

4 cups all purpose flour
½ tsp. sugar
1 tsp. salt
¼ tsp. baking powder
1 Tbsp. shortening
1 ½ cups hot water
4 cups oil

Directions

Mix above ingredients (except water) well. Slowly add hot water until dough comes together. Knead dough until soft and spongy. Form into little balls about 1 ½ inches in diameter. Roll out each ball into an oval about 8 inches wide. Slice in half and then wet sliced edge on both pieces. Hold dough in palm of 1 hand. With other hand bring straight edge together and overlap to form a cone. Fill with vegetable mixture almost to top, moisten the rounded flap with water, fold front and back top edges together by pinching tightly. Sit the "dumpling" upright, cone pointing upward.

Heat oil on high in a wok or deep pan. Reduce heat and slowly fry samosas, turning so they become evenly golden brown and crispy. Serve hot with any sauce or chutney.

Samosa

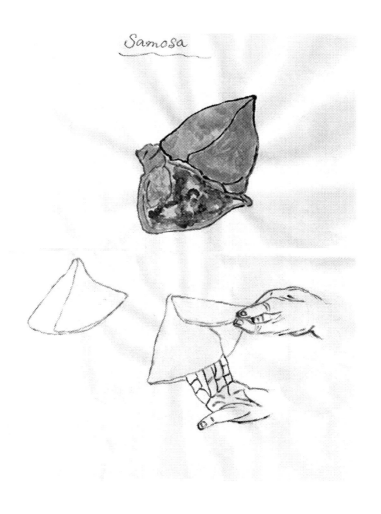

SHAG GUSH WITH LAMB

Ingredients

3 – 4 lbs. lamb, fat removed, cut into small cubes
1 lb. fresh spinach
½ cup oil
½ tsp. whole cumin
2 bay leaves
4 large onions, cut into small pieces
6 garlic cloves, grated
2 Tbsp. sugar
2 Tbsp. grated fresh ginger root
1 Tbsp. turmeric powder
1 Tbsp. chili powder
2 Tbsp. coriander powder
½ cup tomato sauce or 2 fresh tomatoes, chopped
salt to taste
1 tsp. ghee
1 cup sour cream
1 Tbsp. garam masala powder

Directions

Wash lamb and simmer in enough water to cover for ½ hour. Remove stems from spinach leaves and tear into small pieces.

In a deep stew pot, heat oil until just beginning to smoke. Add whole cumin and bay leaves and fry for 30 seconds. Add onions, garlic and sugar. Cook until onions are browned, then add ginger, turmeric powder, chili powder and coriander powder. Fry until golden. Add tomato sauce and mix until oil separates from sauce. Drain lamb and reserve stock. Add meat to sauce. Salt to taste and fry until meat absorbs sauce.

In a very small amount of water, steam spinach for 5 – 10 minutes. Add spinach to meat mixture. Add enough reserved stock to cover meat and simmer until lamb is cooked, about ½ hour. Add ghee, sour cream and garam masala before serving.

This dish may be garnished with sliced or grated hard boiled eggs. Serve with plain rice, pillau or paratha bread.

SHAG GUSH WITH TURKEY

Ingredients

3 – 4 lbs. turkey, cut into small cubes
1 lb. fresh spinach
½ cup oil
½ tsp. whole cumin
2 bay leaves
4 large onions, cut into small pieces
6 garlic cloves, grated
2 Tbsp. sugar
2 Tbsp. grated fresh ginger root
1 Tbsp. turmeric powder
1 Tbsp. chili powder
2 Tbsp. coriander powder
½ cup tomato sauce or 4 fresh tomatoes, chopped
Salt to taste
1 tsp. ghee
1 cup sour cream
1 Tbsp. garam masala powder

Directions

Remove stems from spinach leaves and tear into small pieces.

In a deep stew pot, heat oil until just beginning to smoke. Add whole cumin and bay leaves and fry for 30 seconds. Add onions, garlic and sugar. Cook until onions are browned, then add turkey, ginger, turmeric powder, chili powder and coriander powder. Fry until golden. Add tomato sauce and mix until oil separates from sauce. Salt to taste and fry until meat absorbs sauce.

In a very small amount of water, steam spinach for 5 – 10

minutes. Add spinach to meat mixture. Simmer until turkey is cooked, about ½ hour. Add ghee, sour cream and garam masala before serving.

This dish may be garnished with sliced or grated hard boiled eggs. Serve with plain rice, pillau or paratha bread.

SHAG MATOR
(Chickpeas and Spinach)

Ingredients

$^1/_3$ cup oil
1 tsp. whole cumin
2 large potatoes, cut into cubes
2 cloves of garlic, grated
½ tsp. turmeric powder
1 tsp. Anita's bhaja masala powder
2 tsp. salt
1 tsp. sugar
2 packages frozen chopped spinach, thawed and well drained
2 chilies, cut into quarters
1 lb. can of chickpeas
1 tsp. ghee

Directions

In medium size skillet, heat oil until just beginning to smoke. Then add the whole cumin and fry for a few seconds. Add potatoes and garlic and fry for two minutes. Add the rest of the ingredients, except ghee and mix well. Add spinach, chilies and chickpeas and fry it slowly until potatoes are cooked. Add ghee and serve.

SHAG BHAJI

Ingredients

1 Tbsp. oil
1 tsp. red mustard seeds
1 medium potato, chopped into small pieces
1 small garlic clove, grated
1 tsp. salt
1 tsp. crushed red chili
¼ tsp. turmeric powder
1 lb. chopped spinach (fresh or frozen)

Directions

In a medium frying pan, heat oil on medium heat until just beginning to smoke and then add red mustard seeds. When seeds begin to jump, add potato and garlic. Stir for 1 minute then add salt, crushed chili and turmeric. Mix well. Add fresh spinach, cover and wait a few minutes. Remove cover, spinach will be soft and water will have separated. Fry until water is absorbed. When potatoes have cook through, Shag Bhaji is done.

For frozen spinach, add along with potato and continue to fry until potatoes are cooked. Serve with plain rice and dhal.

SHAHAJANEY CHICKEN BERIANY
(Pillau Rice Cooked with Chicken Pieces)

Ingredients

4 cups basmati rice
1½ cups + 1 Tbsp. ghee
Whole garam masala (4 – 6 bay leaves, 6 – 8 cardamom pods, 2 2" pieces cinnamon stick, 6 – 8 whole cloves and peppercorns)
1 tsp. sugar
2 tsp. salt
2 – 3 lbs. chicken breast and legs cut into pieces
½ cup yogurt
½ tsp. turmeric powder
3 medium onions, sliced lengthwise
¼ cup blanched slivered almonds
¼ cup raw cashew nuts
¼ cup pistachios
1 tsp. grated garlic
2 tsp. grated fresh ginger root
½ tsp. chili powder
1 tsp. cumin powder
½ tsp. ground nutmeg
½ tsp. mace
1 cup heavy cream
½ cup water
6 cups boiling water
½ tsp. saffron soaked in ½ cup warm water
¼ cup white raisins

Directions

Wash and dry the rice. Marinate the rice with ½ cup ghee,

166

whole garam masala pieces, sugar and 1 tsp. salt for one hour.

Wash chicken and remove all fat. Marinate meat with yogurt, 1 tsp. salt and turmeric for 2 hours. In a large sauce pan, heat 1 cup ghee and slowly fry the onions to a light golden brown. Remove the onions with a slotted spoon. In this same pan, fry all the nuts for about 1 minute and set aside. In this same pan, sauté garlic and ginger for 1 – 2 minutes before adding the meat. Brown the meat for 10 – 15 minutes until tender. Then add chili powder, cumin, nutmeg and mace, stirring well. Pour in ½ cup heavy cream and ½ cup water; cover pan and simmer about 10 minutes.

In a large deep casserole dish, add 1 Tbsp. ghee and grease well. Layer $^1/_3$ of the marinated rice on the bottom of the casserole dish. Next a layer of half of the meat, alternating layers ending with rice. Then add boiling water and ½ cup heavy cream. Bring to a boil on the stove top, then place dish in oven or continue to simmer dish on stove top.

When rice is fluffy garnish with saffron mixture. When ready to serve, garnish top with onions, almonds, cashews, pistachios and raisins.

SHAHAJANEY CHICKEN KUFTA

Ingredients

3 – 4 lbs. ground, boned and skinned chicken
4 large onions, grated
½ cup unseasoned bread crumbs
2 eggs
3 tsp. salt
1 Tbsp. grated fresh ginger root
½ tsp. chili powder
1½ cups oil
¼ cup ghee
½ tsp. whole cumin
8 – 10 cardamom pods
6 – 8 whole cloves
6 – 8 peppercorns
1 2" piece cinnamon stick, cut up
1 tsp. grated garlic
1 tsp. sugar
2 tsp. coriander powder
1 tsp. garam masala powder
½ tsp. nutmeg
2 large tomatoes, diced
1 cup blanched almonds
1 cup sour cream
¼ tsp. saffron, soaked in ½ cup hot water
Fresh cilantro leaves

Directions

In a mixing bowl, combine chicken, $^1/_3$ of the onion, bread crumbs, eggs, 1 tsp. salt, 1 tsp. grated ginger, ¼ tsp. chili powder. After mixing well, shape into plumb sized balls. Heat 1 cup oil in a frying pan and fry a few balls at a time until lightly browned. Place fried balls in a casserole dish.

In a saucepan, heat remaining oil and ghee. Fry whole spices for 30 seconds. Add remaining grated onion, ginger, garlic and sugar. Sauté 8 – 10 minutes until lightly browned. Then add all powdered spices and tomatoes. Cook slowly for 10 – 15 minutes.

While the sauce is cooking, add the almonds, sour cream and soaked saffron to a blender and blend well. Add this mixture into the sauce and mix well. Pour the creamy sauce over the chicken balls. Bake covered in a 400° oven for 20 minutes. Top with cilantro leaves. This makes a delicious main dish.

SHAHAJANEY LAMB BERIANY
(Pillau Rice Cooked with Lamb Pieces)

Ingredients

4 cups basmati rice
2 tsp. salt
8 ½ cups water
2 – 3 lbs. lamb, cut into 1" pieces (preferably leg of lamb)
½ cup yogurt
½ tsp. turmeric powder
1½ cups ghee
3 medium onions, sliced thin lengthwise
¼ cup blanched slivered almonds
¼ cup raw cashew nuts
¼ cup pistachios
1 tsp. grated garlic
2 tsp. grated fresh ginger root
1 tsp. sugar
½ tsp. chili powder
1 tsp. cumin powder
½ tsp. ground nutmeg
½ tsp. mace
½ cup heavy cream
Whole garam masala (4 – 6 bay leaves, 6 – 8 cardamom pods, 2 2" pieces cinnamon stick, 6 – 8 whole cloves and peppercorns)
½ tsp. saffron soaked in ½ cup warm water
¼ cup white raisins

Directions

Partially boil washed rice with 1 tsp. salt in 8 cups water (boil briskly about 10 minutes). Drain in strainer and set aside.

Wash lamb and remove all fat. Marinate meat with yogurt, 1 tsp. salt and turmeric for 2 hours. In a large sauce pan, heat 1 cup ghee and slowly fry the onions to a light golden brown. Remove the onions with a slotted spoon. In this same pan, fry all the nuts for about 1 minute and set aside. In this same pan, sauté garlic, ginger and sugar for 1 – 2 minutes before adding the meat. Brown the meat for 10 – 15 minutes until tender. Then add chili powder, cumin, nutmeg and mace, stirring well. Pour in heavy cream and ½ cup water; cover pan and simmer about 10 minutes.

In a small sauce pan, heat remaining ghee and brown whole garam masala spices. Grease a large casserole dish well with ½ of the ghee mixture. Layer $^1/_3$ of the cooked rice on the bottom of the casserole dish, next a layer of ½ of the meat, then another layer of rice. Sprinkle with remaining ghee mixture, then layer remaining meat and top with remaining rice. Pour the saffron mixture over the top layer of rice. Pour the remaining sauce from the meat along the sides of the casserole. Cover tightly and bake for 20 minutes.

When ready to serve, garnish top with onions, almonds, cashews, pistachios and raisins.

SHAHEY CHICKEN
(Spicy Sour Cream Chicken)

Ingredients

2 cups coarsely chopped onions
6 garlic cloves
2 inch piece fresh ginger root, peeled
1 fresh tomato, chopped
½ cup oil
Whole garam masala – few pieces cardamom, cloves, bay leaves and peppercorns
2 tsp. salt
1 tsp. sugar
2 tsp. coriander powder
2 tsp. chili powder
4 - 5 lbs. chicken breasts and thighs, skinned, boned and cut into 1 inch pieces
1 cup sour cream (regular or light)
½ cup water
2 tsp. garam masala powder
1 Tbsp. ghee
Fresh cilantro leaves

Directions

Blend onions, garlic, ginger and tomato in a blender and set aside.

In a large saucepan, heat oil until just beginning to smoke. Add garam masala pieces and fry for 30 seconds. Add the blended onion mixture then sprinkle with salt and sugar. Stir and continue to cook for 6 – 8 minutes or until the oil and onions separate. Add coriander powder and chili powder and mix well. Add chicken and stir for 10 minutes on medium heat. Add sour cream and water. Cover and cook for 15 minutes on low heat. When chicken is tender, but not shredded, add garam masala powder and ghee.

Serve warm and garnish with fresh cilantro leaves. This dish is excellent with Indian bread or rice.

SHANAR ZILAPY

Ingredients

1 drop of ghee
1 gallon milk
1 cup lemon juice
1 cup Bisquick®
1 cup non-fat dry milk
¼ tsp. baking powder
½ tsp. ground nutmeg
¼ cup melted butter
4 cups vegetable shortening
4 cups sugar
4 cups water

Directions

In a large pot add drop of ghee to prevent sticking. Add milk and heat on medium until reaching a foaming boil. Gradually add lemon juice while stirring. The milk will separate into a cheese and whey. Line a colander with cheesecloth and pour contents of pot into it. Press liquid out of mixture then wrap cheesecloth around cheese and let sit for at least an hour to allow further drying.

Make smooth dough by mixing cheese, Bisquick, dry milk, baking powder, nutmeg and butter. This can best be done on a flat surface using your hands to mix. Refrigerate dough for 1 hour. Take plum sized pieces of dough and roll into long, round strips 9 – 10 inches in length. Form into pretzel shapes. Melt shortening in a pan and deep fry pretzels until golden brown. Do not fry too fast – it should take 8 – 10 minutes per batch. Drain on paper towels.

Bring sugar and water to a boil and continue to boil for 5

minutes. While zilapies and syrup are still hot, drop all zilapies into syrup to soak. Remove from heat and allow syrup to cool before removing zilapies. Serve warm or cool with coffee.

® Bisquick is a registered trademark of General Mills, Inc.

SHANDESH
(Sweetened Cheese)

Ingredients

1 tsp. plus 1 drop of ghee
½ gallon milk
$1/_3$ cup lemon juice
1 cup sugar
Rose water or grated orange rind

Directions

In a large pot add drop of ghee to prevent sticking. Add milk and heat on medium until reaching a foaming boil. Gradually add lemon juice while stirring. The milk should curdle with a greenish liquid rising to the surface. If so, the cheese is done. If not, drain into a colander lined with cheesecloth. Press liquid out of mixture, then let drain until cheese is dry. This produces a very mild cheese. To sweeten, add sugar and mix well by mashing until a smooth paste is produced.

In a medium pot, melt 1 tsp. ghee. Add cheese mixture stirring briefly. Cook for a few minutes then add flavoring such as rose water or grated orange rind. After 5 minutes, remove from heat. Form into balls and serve warm or press into small, lightly oiled molds and serve cold in attractive shapes.

SHRIMP MALAI CURRY

Ingredients

½ cup ghee
few whole pieces of garam masala
1 tsp. salt
1 tsp. sugar
1 large onion, finely chopped
2 Tbsp. grated fresh ginger root
1 tsp. chopped fresh garlic
1 cup chopped tomatoes or tomato sauce
1 tsp. chili powder
2 tsp. tandoori masala powder
2 Tbsp. oil
2 lbs. fresh shrimp peeled and deveined
¼ tsp. turmeric powder
¼ tsp. garlic powder
1 tsp. salt
1 cup peeled, fresh coconut pieces and 2 cups half & half processed in blender to a paste
½ cup water
1 tsp. garam masala powder

Directions

Warm ghee in a heavy sauce pan. Place whole garam masala pieces, salt, sugar, onion, ginger and garlic into pan and fry until lightly browned. Add tomato, chili powder and tandoori powder to pan. Stir sauce for about 5 minutes. In the meantime, add oil to a small frying pan, heat and sauté shrimp with turmeric, garlic powder and salt until pink. Then add coconut mixture, water and garam masala powder along with shrimp to the sauce. Bring to a boil and simmer for 1 – 2 minutes. Shrimp should be nicely coated with sauce.

This shrimp can be served with any rice dish. The coconut sauce is mouthwatering!

The coconut paste can be purchased as a coconut cream powder in any Asian market, just mix with 1 cup of milk.

Sambar Masala Powder

¼ tsp. compounded asafoetidahing (hing)
1 tsp. cumin powder
1 tsp. coriander powder
½ tsp. chili powder ?
¼ tsp. black ground pepper

Combine

Ghee
(Clarified Butter)

2 lbs. unsalted butter
1 cup whole milk
Few pieces bay leaves
$1/8$ tsp. saffron

Simmer all of the ingredients in a medium sized pot on very low heat for 1 hour. The mixture will separate into a transparent, light orange colored liquid on the top and browned solids on the bottom. Skim the transparent liquid off the top and pour through a fine strainer. This is ghee and must be refrigerated.

SPICY ALOO DOM

Ingredients

2 lb. new potatoes (plum sized red)
1 onion, chopped
1 inch of ginger root, grated
1 clove garlic
1 small green chili
½ cup oil
1 tsp. whole cumin
1 bay leaf
1 cinnamon stick
6 whole cardamom
6 whole cloves
1 Tbsp. sugar
2 Tbsp. yogurt
½ cup crushed tomato
2 tsp. garam masala powder
1 tsp. ghee
chopped fresh cilantro

Directions

Boil potatoes in their skins, cool, peel and set aside. In a blender, mix onions, ginger, garlic and green chili then set aside. Heat oil in a pan and brown the potatoes; remove to a serving bowl. Add cumin, bay leaf, cinnamon, cardamom and cloves and fry for a few minutes. Add onion mixture and lightly brown. Add sugar, then yogurt 1 Tbsp. at a time until well mixed. Add the prepared potato mixture and tomato and cook adding water if necessary. Remove to serving bowl and sprinkle with garam masala, ghee and chopped fresh cilantro. Best if served with poori.

SPICY CATFISH ROAST

Ingredients

2 – 3 1 lb. whole cat fish, scaled and gutted
1 Tbsp. lemon juice
1 tsp. salt
¼ cup olive oil
1 tsp. whole cumin
1 tsp. garlic paste
2 tsp. ginger paste
1 tsp. turmeric powder
2 tsp. red chili powder
2 tsp. coriander powder
2 tsp. Anita's bhaja masala powder
4 green chilies, sliced
A few coriander leaves

Directions

In a baking dish, marinate fish in lemon juice and salt. Let this stand for 30 minutes.

In a small frying pan, heat oil until just beginning to smoke. Add whole cumin and allow to spatter for a few seconds. Then add garlic paste and fry for 20 seconds. Add ginger paste and remaining spices and blend well into oil. Cook for about 1 minute. With a spatula, thoroughly coat both sides of the fish with the cooked spice mixture.

With olive oil, generously grease a flat baking pan. Place fish on pan side by side and bake in a 400° oven for 30 minutes. Fish will be golden brown and crispy.

Present on a platter garnished with green chilies and coriander leaves. Serve with fried potato sticks. Serves 4 – 5.

STUFFED EGGPLANT

Ingredients

12 small eggplants
1 cup peanuts
1 cup roasted chhola dhal
½ cup crushed fresh coconut
½ cup olive oil
1 tsp. red mustard seeds
¼ tsp. hing
2 tsp. chili powder
2 tsp. Anita's masala powder
1 tsp. coriander powder
2 tsp. salt
1 cup sliced onions

Directions

Clean the surface of each eggplant and cut the tops off. Scoop out the flesh and discard. Mix peanuts, chhola dhal and coconut in a blender. Heat 1 Tbsp. of the oil in a skillet until just beginning to smoke, then fry mustard seeds and hing for 30 seconds. Add the blended mixture along with 1 tsp. chili powder, 1 tsp. Anita's masala, ½ tsp. coriander powder and 1 tsp. salt. Mix well and cook for 1 minute.

Stuff each with the peanut mixture and replace the top. Heat the remaining oil until just beginning to smoke. Fry the remaining spices. Then add the onions. Carefully lay the stuffed eggplants on top of the onions and cook on low heat for about 20 minutes while turning each eggplant carefully until well cooked.

TANDOORI CHICKEN

Chicken Ingredients

4 lbs chicken legs and thighs
4 garlic cloves
2 onions, cut up
2 tsp. grated fresh ginger root
1 tsp. chili powder
2 tsp. coriander powder
1 tsp. cumin powder
2 tsp. tandoori masala powder
1 tsp. garam masala powder
1 tsp red food coloring
1 tsp. yellow food coloring
4 Tbsp. plain yogurt
2 Tbsp. vinegar
2 Tbsp. oil
2 tsp. salt
1 large onion, sliced and lemon slices for garnish

Directions

Peel skin off chicken, wash and set aside. Place all remaining ingredients (except onion and lemon slices) into a blender and blend at medium speed until well mixed. Dip chicken pieces, one by one, into the mixture and lay on a baking sheet. Refrigerate for about 1 day to marinate.

Preheat oven to 400° and bake 35 – 40 minutes or until well cooked. If barbecue is preferred, follow same instruction, but grill chicken for about 15 minutes each side. Decorate this delicious dish with fresh onions and lemon slices. Serve with fried rice.

TARKA DHAL

Ingredients

2 cups green muge
8 cups water
¼ cup oil
1 tsp. whole cumin
A few pieces of bay leaf, cardamom pods and cinnamon sticks
1 cup fresh coconut, cut into pieces
2 large tomatoes, chopped
2 tsp. grated fresh ginger root
3 tsp. salt
2 tsp. sugar
1 tsp. chili powder
1 tsp. ghee
2 tsp. garam masala powder
Fresh cilantro leaves

Directions

Wash muge well and cook in water about 1 hour (until muge are well cooked – almost mushy). In small skillet heat oil then add whole cumin, bay leaf, cardamom pods, cinnamon sticks and coconut pieces and fry about 2 minutes. Then add tomatoes, ginger, salt, sugar, chili powder and mix well. Add this mixture to the cooked muge, combine well and cook slowly for 10 minutes. Add ghee and garam masala powder. Top with fresh cilantro.

This green muge dish is delicious with rice, naan bread or parathas.

VEGETABLE CHOPS

Ingredients

½ cup oil
2 large onions, chopped
½ tsp. chili powder
1 tsp. cumin powder
1 tsp. garam masala powder
1 tsp. turmeric powder
2 tsp. salt
1 tsp. sugar
1 tsp. grated fresh ginger root
1 large tomato, chopped
2 cups finely chopped carrots, green beans, peas and beets
1 cup water
¼ cup raisins
½ cup peanuts
2 lbs. potatoes, boiled and mashed
1 Tbsp. lemon juice
2 eggs, beaten
2 cups bread crumbs

Directions

Heat 2 Tbsp. of the oil in a small pan. Fry the onions until they are lightly browned. Add the chili, cumin, garam masala, turmeric, salt, sugar, ginger and tomatoes and mix well. Add the chopped carrots, beans, peas and beets to the mixture and cook for about 20 minutes on low heat. While the mixture is cooking, add the cup of water. Once vegetables are well cooked, add raisins, peanuts, mashed potatoes and lemon juice and mix all the ingredients well.

Let the mixture cool. Take a large Tbsp. of the mixture at a time and form individual patties in the shape of a 2 inch oval. Dip one chop at a time into the eggs, and then dredge in bread crumbs. Heat remaining oil in a frying pan. Fry chops until they are dark brown.

VEGETABLE KUFTA

Ingredients

Desired amount of:
  Potatoes
  Peas
  Carrots
  Beans
  Pumpkin
  Beets
1 tsp. chili powder
2 tsp. cumin powder
2 tsp. turmeric powder
1 tsp. garam masala powder
1 cup graham flour or pancake mix
¾ cup oil
1 tsp. whole cumin
2 large onions, chopped
2 large fresh tomatoes or ½ cup tomato sauce
2 tsp. grated fresh ginger root
4 tsp. salt
2 tsp. sugar
1 cup water
2 tsp. ghee

Directions

Boil all vegetables in list. Drain and mash into a large bowl. Add half the measurement of each powdered ingredient and the graham flour. Mix until well blended. Make ping pong sized balls out of mixture.

Heat oil in a frying pan and fry balls until lightly browned. Set aside. In the same pan, brown the whole cumin, then add the onions and fry until browned. Add the remaining ingredients except for remaining garam masala, water and ghee. Fry until a creamy sauce forms. Add water and the balls to the sauce and cook about 5 minutes. Add the garam masala and ghee. Serve with rice or paratha.

VEGETABLE NABRATAN

Ingredients

½ cup oil
1 tsp. black cumin seeds
1 cup chopped onion
4 medium potatoes, cut into ½" pieces
1 cup ½" pieces of sweet potatoes
1 cup chopped beets
½ cauliflower head, broken into 1 – 1 ½" pieces
2 tsp. salt
2 tsp. sugar
1 tsp. crushed red chili
½ tsp. turmeric powder
1 Tbsp. Anita's masala powder
1 cup chopped tomato
2 – 3 green chilies, sliced
½ cup grated fresh coconut
1 cup cut green beans
1 cup chopped carrots
2 cups sliced butternut squash
1 cup green peas
½ cup water

Directions

In a deep, medium sized frying pan, heat oil on medium until just beginning to smoke. Add black cumin, onions, potatoes, sweet potatoes and beets. Stir for 1 minute then add cauliflower, salt and sugar. Continue to stir for 1 minute more.

Push vegetables to the sides, making space in the center. Add remaining spices and fry for 1 minute. Add tomatoes, chilies and coconut then mix well. Add beans, carrots, squash and green peas to combine with all ingredients in pan. Add ½ cup water and cook for an additional 10 minutes or until vegetables are well cooked but not mushy.

This delicious mix of vegetables can be served with luchis or paratha along with chutney.

YAKHNI PILLAU

Rice Ingredients

2 ½ cups Basmati rice
¼ cup ghee
4 bay leaves
4 – 6 pieces whole cardamom
a few pieces of cinnamon stick
8 black pepper corns
2 Tbsp. sugar
1 tsp. salt
½ cup raisins
¼ cup sliced almond
¼ cup cream
$\frac{1}{8}$ tsp saffron

Directions

Wash rice, drain and spread on paper towel to dry completely.

Place rice in a medium size pot. In a small pan, heat ghee and whole spices, then pour over rice. Add sugar and salt. Let rice marinate for 2 hours.

Yakhni Water Ingredients

6 cups water
1 tsp. salt
4 – 5 pieces bay leaves
2 – 3 inch piece of cinnamon stick
8 – 10 pieces whole cardamom
2 inch piece of fresh ginger root cut into pieces

4 – 5 dry red chilies
¼ cup whole channa dhal
2 Tbsp. whole cumin

Directions

In a 8 quart pot, bring water and salt to a boil. In a clean cheese cloth, tie up all remaining ingredients and drop into boiling water and bring to a simmer. Cover and continue to simmer for 2 hours. Will yield approximately 3 ½ cups of Yakhni water.

Pour yakhni water into marinated rice mixture. Add raisins and almonds. Bring to a boil until almost all water is absorbed. Pour cream on top and sprinkle with saffron. Gently fold rice a few times, cover and cook on low heat until rice grains are separated and fluffy.

Pillau is ready for serving.

YAKHNI PILLAU WITH LAMB

Marinade Ingredients

1 cup plain yogurt
1 cup crushed onion
2 tsp. salt
1 tsp. grated garlic

Ingredients

2 – 3 lbs. lamb or goat meat, cut into 1 ½ inch pieces
½ cup olive oil
6 cups water
½ cup whole garam masala pieces
½ cup ghee
1 tsp. whole white cumin
1 cup chopped onions
2 Tbsp. grated fresh ginger root
1 tsp. grated garlic
1 tsp. chili powder
1 tsp. salt
¼ tsp. saffron
1 large tomato, chopped
2 cups basmati rice, washed, drained and spread out on a dish cloth to dry
½ cup skinless, slivered almonds
4 hard boiled eggs, sliced in half

Directions

Combine first 4 ingredients, add to meat, stir well to coat and marinate over night.

In a medium sized pan, add ¼ cup oil and heat until just beginning to smoke. Add ¼ cup whole garam masala spices and brown. Add water and bring to a boil. Add marinated meat, cover and simmer for at least 1 hour or until meat is tender.

In an 8 qt. pan, heat remaining oil and ¼ cup ghee. Fry remaining whole garam masala pieces, cumin, onion, grated ginger and garlic. Then add chili powder and salt.

Remove meat pieces from the stock and set aside. Add remaining ghee, saffron, tomato and rice. Stir gently and brown the mixture for 3 – 4 minutes. Replace meat and add fried spices. Bring all of this to a boil for 3 – 4 minutes. When liquid is reduced by half, cover and simmer on very low heat until rice is fluffy.

While meat mixture is simmering, sauté almonds in a small amount of oil until golden brown. Place dish on a flat platter and top with almonds and hard boiled eggs.

Serve this dish with cucumber raita and a selection of pickles.

YELLOW SPLIT PEA DHAL
(with Fresh Squash and Green Beans)

Ingredients

1 ½ cup yellow split peas
4 cups water
2 tsp. salt
$^1/_8$ tsp. baking soda
¼ tsp. turmeric powder
1 Tbsp. sugar
¼ cup oil
1 tsp. whole black cumin
2 pieces of bay leaf
½ lb. green beans, cut into 1" pieces
3 small green squash, peeled in alternating stripes, cut in half and 1" sliced
1 tsp. crushed red pepper
2 tsp. grated fresh ginger root
2 tsp. ghee
2 tsp. Anita's bhaja masala
2 – 3 pieces slices green chili
½ cup fresh cilantro leaves

Directions

Clean and pick over yellow split peas. Add to a pan along with 4 cups water and bring to a boil. Add 1 ½ tsp. salt, baking soda and turmeric powder. Simmer until the peas are soft. Add sugar while cooking the dhal.

In a separate frying pan, heat oil until just beginning to smoke then add black cumin and bay leaf. Fry until leaves are brown then add bin, squash, remaining salt, crushed red pepper and ginger. Stir for 2 minutes then add mixture to the dhal. Boil dhal mixture on low heat until the vegetables are very tender. Add ghee and Anita's bhaja masala. Stir well. Dhal is ready to garnish with green chilies and cilantro.

This dhal can be served as a side dish with plain rice in a soup bowl. This is an excellent full vegetarian meal.

ZILAPY

Ingredients

2 cups all purpose flour
1 cup rice flour
½ tsp. quick rising yeast
½ tsp. yellow food coloring
2 cups plus 2 Tbsp. water
4 cups oil
2 cups sugar

Directions

Add flours, yeast, food coloring and 2 cups water to a large mixing bowl and mix well. Cover for 2 hours.

Pour dough mixture into a squeeze bottle. In a large frying pan heat 4 cups of oil until very hot. With the squeeze bottle, create 2 inch wide spirals in the heated oil. Fry for 1 – 2 minutes then remove to a paper towel to drain.

In a small frying pan, heat and mix sugar with 2 Tbsp. water to make thick syrup. Spread warm zilapies on a tray and spread a layer of syrup over the top. Allow to cool, the zilapies will be nice and crispy.

MENUS

MENU

Samosas

Chicken Korma

Rice Pillau

Aloo-Kopi-r Dalna
(Cauliflower and Potato Curry)

Pineapple Chutney

Gulab Jamun

MENU

Moghuli Kabab

Lamb Roganjosh

Tarka Dhal

Naan Bread

Plain Rice

Mixed Fruit Chutney

Payesh
(Rice Pudding)

MENU

Fish Chops

Buttered Chicken

Bhindi Bhaji
(Fried Okra)

Rice Pillau
(see menu 1 for recipe)

Mango Chutney

Rash Malai

MENU

Vegetable Chops

Parathas

Royal Moghuli Lamb Roast
(with Chiffon Rice)

Palak Paneer
(Spinach Paneer)

Dahi Raita with Cucumber

Mango Chutney
(see menu 3 for recipe)

Malpoa

MENU

Aloo Chops
(Potato Patties)

Kachuri
(Bread Stuffed with Green Peas)

Spicy Aloo Dom

Shrimp Malai Curry

Yakhni Pillau

Chopped Cucumber Salad

Plum Chutney

Rose Water Kulfi

MENU

Eggplant Begún Varthá

Paneer Kufta

Paneer Pillau

Roast Muge Dhal
(with Cauliflower & Potato)

Mango Chutney

Rash Malai

MENU

Vegetable Chops

Luchi

Palak Paneer
(Spinach Paneer)

Plain Rice

Sambar Dhal

Tomato Chutney

Malpoa

Printed in the United States
99368LV00005B/128/A